Awaken

Reviving Your Soul in the Treasure of Christ

A Study of Philippians

Joy Kats

Awaken: Reviving Your Soul in the Treasure of Christ
Copyright © 2022 Joy Kats
All rights reserved.

Unless otherwise noted, Scripture quotations are from the ESV® Bible (The Holy Bible, English Standard Version®), copyright © 2001 by Crossway, a publishing ministry of Good News Publishers. Used by permission. All rights reserved. The ESV text may not be quoted in any publication made available to the public by a Creative Commons license. The ESV may not be translated into any other language.

Scripture quotations marked (NLT) are taken from the *Holy Bible,* New Living Translation, copyright ©1996, 2004, 2015 by Tyndale House Foundation. Used by permission of Tyndale House Publishers, Carol Stream, Illinois 60188. All rights reserved.

Editor: Cherry Lyn Hoffner
Cover Design: Courtney Satterblom

ISBN: 978-1-955309-18-9

DEDICATION

To all those who walk with me, pray with me, challenge me, and point me to Jesus every day: I am forever grateful for your partnership in the gospel.

To all those I am privileged to serve and teach: I am so thankful to be partakers of God's amazing grace together.

To Christ Jesus, my Lord: thank you for awakening my heart to the absolute treasure you are! I'm all yours, now and forever.

CONTENTS

	About the Author		1
	A Note from Joy		2
	Maximizing this Study		5
Week One	Introduction & Greeting	Phil. 1:1–2	9
Week Two	Awaken to the Fellowship of Christ	Phil. 1:3–11	19
Week Three	Awaken to the Satisfaction of Christ	Phil. 1:12–30	33
Week Four	Awaken to the Mind of Christ	Phil. 2:1–11	47
Week Five	Awaken to the Work of Christ	Phil. 2:12–30	63
Week Six	Awaken to the Worth of Christ	Phil. 3:1–11	77
Week Seven	Awaken to the Prize of Christ	Phil. 3:12–4:1	93
Week Eight	Awaken to the Joy of Christ	Phil. 4:2–9	107
Week Nine	Awaken to the Provision of Christ	Phil. 4:10–23	123
Week Ten	The Absolute Treasure of Christ		137
	Awaken My Heart		143
	ESV Scriptures		145
	Word Study Guide		151
	Notes		154

ABOUT THE AUTHOR

Joy Kats is first and foremost, a beloved daughter of God. She and her husband Marc have been married for 27 years. They have a daughter, Alaina; son-in-law, Collin; and twin sons, Ethan and Tucker. Joy has been writing for over three decades and has nearly twenty years of ministry experience.

A Bible college graduate, Joy has continued to devour God's Word, deepening her faith, and growing her passion to disciple and encourage others in the body of Christ. Joy is the author of *Free Indeed: Uncovering the Glorious Freedom of Grace* and the *Free Indeed Companion Book*. She is also a Bible teacher, and retreat and ministry speaker.

Awakened by the treasure of Christ in her own life, Joy has an intense desire to point others to Jesus. She seeks to walk with them as their hearts are awakened and their souls revived by the satisfaction found only in Christ. One of Joy's greatest passions is for believers to experience together the treasures of abundant, eternal life on this side of heaven. *Awaken* is the second Bible study Joy has written.

Joy would love to connect with you at joykats.com or on Instagram @joykatswrites and Facebook @Joy Kats, Writer & Speaker.

A NOTE FROM JOY

Dear Friends,

Have you ever wondered what the world would look like if God's church was truly awake to the things of heaven and desperate to make much of Christ? What if we overlooked denominational differences and set aside divisions; if we walked in true fellowship with one another, pursuing Christ in love and unity? Can you just imagine the body of believers living zealous lives with hearts ablaze by the transforming power of the gospel? It impassions my heart and stirs my soul to think that we could actually be everything God designed and destined for us to be as a people, as His beloved bride.

Too often, though, as we move through life, we find ourselves distracted and comfortable, complacent and lukewarm in our faith. Sure, Jesus is part of life, but He ceases to be our center of life. We lose our passion for the gospel, sometimes becoming apathetic toward the things of God. We might even fall asleep at the wheel on our journey with Jesus.

But I have good news: God is the God of revival. And friends, it's time to wake up! It's time to rise up and step up to His kingdom call—not to revitalize religion but to revive our souls in Christ Himself. To be revived means we are restored from an inactive state, filled with new energy and strength for life. When we awaken, we are roused from our slumber and our hearts stir with an unmistakable ability to enjoy the goodness of God in every moment. This, sweet friends, is abundant life! And it begins with you ... and me—each one of God's people intentionally opening our minds and hearts to personally experience the revival of our souls as we awaken (maybe for the first time) to the fullness of God and the absolute treasure of Christ.

Awaken offers a fresh perspective on the book of Philippians. While often known as a book about joy, this New Testament letter is not only about experiencing joy in the Christian life; it's also about better understanding and treasuring the One who fills us with such joy.

Every element of this study is designed to get you deeply into God's Word for the purpose of getting His Word deeply into you. I challenge you to dig in and go deep. Pray and ponder. Grapple and grow. The gospel is the power of God for salvation for all who believe, and one day every knee will bow and every tongue will confess that Jesus Christ is Lord. My hope is that as we work through this study together, you will awaken to the fellowship of Christ, the satisfaction of Christ, and the mind of Christ. I pray you will awaken to the work and worth of Christ, the prize of Christ, the joy of Christ, and the provision of Christ. My prayer is for you to join Paul in counting everything as loss compared to the surpassing worth of knowing Jesus Christ.

I have been praying for you as I have been writing this study and continue to pray for every person who works through these pages. I pray the same for you as Paul prayed for the church at Philippi: that "your love will overflow more and more, and that you will keep on growing in knowledge and understanding. For I want you to understand what really matters, so that you may live pure and blameless lives until the day of Christ's return. May you always be filled with the fruit of your salvation—the righteous character produced in your life by Jesus Christ—for this will bring much glory and praise to God" (Phil. 1:9—11 NLT).

When awakened individuals come together, joining spiritual forces with red hot faith and empowered by the Spirit of God, we as God's church can undoubtedly change the world! So whether you have been journeying with Jesus for days or decades, may you awaken to the fullness of God and be revived by the absolute treasure of Christ—for His glory and praise!

In His Love,

Joy Kats

MAXIMIZING THIS STUDY

This inductive Bible study includes three main parts that can be divided and used for either individual study or group study:
- Daily Study
- Teaching
- Small Group Discussion and Prayer

DAILY STUDY: WHAT'S THE POINT?
The goals for the daily personal study include the following:
- reading the Scripture carefully and repeatedly for all it's worth, noting words, tense, and the point of view from which it is written
- focusing your mind and opening your heart to biblical truth
- gaining a better understanding of what Scripture says
- learning how to live it out practically and effectively

Each week after the Introduction and Greeting, the given Scripture for the week will be separated into three smaller passages. The weekly study material is divided into four days, but you are encouraged to work through it at your own pace. The study of each Scripture text will include the following steps:

1. **TAKE IT IN:** read and re-read the book; read the weekly passage
2. **WRITE IT DOWN:** mark repeated words, write out the memory verse
3. **THINK IT THROUGH:** study Greek words and cross-references, process the text
4. **STORE IT UP:** ponder, reflect, memorize
5. **MAKE IT COUNT:** apply

Steps 1 and 2 are designed to help you know what the Scripture says.
Steps 3 and 4 are designed to help you understand what the Scripture means.
Step 5 is designed to help you allow the Scripture to change you as you live it out.

KEY ELEMENTS OF THIS STUDY

Prayer: Always begin and end your study time in prayer, asking God to reveal Himself powerfully through His Word.

Repeated Reading of the Passage: You will be regularly and repeatedly reading the passage. You will also read from several different Bible translations (as instructed in the study material). This has proven to be very helpful in understanding the text. A printed copy of the English Standard Version can be found in the back of this book. You will also need a print or digital copy (check out BibleGateway.com) of the Amplified Version and the New Living Translation to reference as you study.

Key Words/Themes: Identifying repeated words or ideas reinforces the focus and themes throughout the study. Please plan to have highlighters on hand as these will be useful for marking key words and themes throughout the text.

Word Studies: Understanding the original language is helpful for better understanding the text. For these you will need access to Strong's Concordance and/or BlueLetterBible.org. You can also use the word study guide in the back of this study book.

Cross-References: Referencing other Scripture passages helps awaken us to the consistency of God's character throughout His Word and allows us to interpret Scripture with Scripture.

Scripture Memory: The memorization of Scripture is important, but something we don't often do as adults. Each lesson includes a verse you will be challenged to write out and memorize throughout the week.

Praying with Joy: Paul opens his letter to the Philippians with prayers of joy and continues this theme throughout. After each week of reading and studying, I invite you to join me (Joy ☺) in joyful prayer and continual pursuit of Christ as we grow in Him and seek to know Him more.

TEACHING: WHAT'S THE POINT?

To maximize this study, I strongly encourage you to include a teaching time that follows the personal weekly study time. Go to joykats.com for access to the video teachings of each week's lesson. Some church groups may also provide live teaching each week when you meet together. Another option for group or individual study is to do additional research on your own using Bible commentaries or listening to sermons or other teachings on the text. I urge you to wait to do this until after you've completed the study material, giving yourself opportunity to dig into the Scripture and wrestle with it on your own first. The goal for the teaching time is to gain a fuller understanding of the Scripture you've studied. As the teacher shares insight gained from additional research and resources, it will help you know how to apply biblical truth to your life today.

SMALL GROUP DISCUSSION & PRAYER: WHAT'S THE POINT?
If you are participating in a group study, small group discussion and prayer time will be the final component of each week's lesson. After working through the study material and listening to the teaching or doing additional study on your own, small groups will spend time discussing what you have heard and/or studied. The goals are to discuss what you have learned, encourage one another by sharing personal experiences and insights, pray for one another, and grow together in the grace and knowledge of our Lord and Savior Jesus Christ.

A couple more things to note:

Even though you will be reading from several translations of Scripture, all the study questions correlate to the ESV, unless otherwise noted.

It's important to remember that this study is available to anyone wanting to learn more about God's Word and what it means for our lives. That means some may be newer in the faith while others are veterans in the faith. For this reason, you will encounter questions with varying degrees of depth. Having to think through and write out answers to questions (regardless of where we are in our faith journey) forces us to remind ourselves what we believe and why we believe it, thus allowing the truth to revive our own souls.

"Awake, my soul and sing
Of Him who died for thee
And hail Him as thy matchless King
Thru all eternity."

"Crown Him With Many Crowns"[1]

Week One

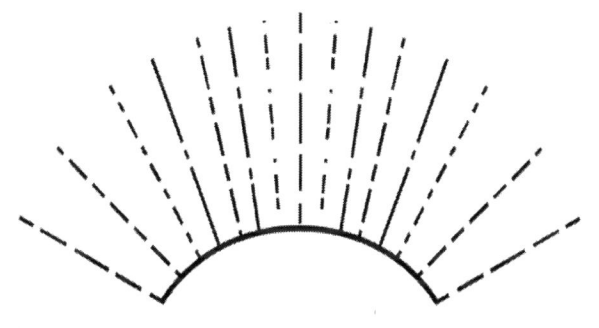

INTRODUCTION AND GREETING

Philippians 1:1–2

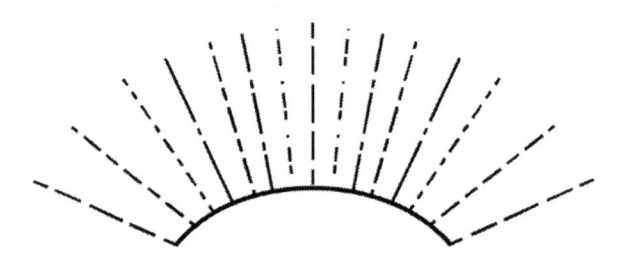

INTRODUCTION TO THIS STUDY

As you begin, I encourage you to think about why you've chosen to work through this study. You have said "no" to something else in order to say "yes" to this—why?

Take a few moments to complete the following sentences.

    I have chosen to be part of this study because . . .

    My goals are . . .

No matter what your season or stage of life or faith, I trust God to meet you right where you are and teach you more about Himself and His Word. He longs to be in intimate relationship with you, and I believe He will bless you for making this study a priority in your life. Thinking through and writing down your goals as you begin will help keep you on track as you work through this study.

This lesson only: if you are utilizing the teaching component, you will complete this week's study as you listen to the teaching. All remaining study lessons will be completed before the teaching time.

INTRODUCTION TO PHILIPPIANS

When studying a book of the Bible, it is vital to know its context and history. So we begin with information and background details that are necessary for understanding the dynamic of this short New Testament book. We will ask and answer a series of important questions that will help determine the history and context of Philippians. Let's get started!

It was customary for first-century writers to open with a salutation that includes the name of the author, the name of the recipient or group of recipients, and a short greeting. We find this to be true at the beginning of Philippians:

"Paul and Timothy, servants of Christ Jesus, To all the saints in Christ Jesus who are at Philippi, with the overseers and deacons . . ." (1:1)

1. Who is the author of this book?

If you're not familiar with this person, take a few moments to read Acts 8-9. Not only will you better understand the author of this book, but you will also be encouraged by the power of God who works in the lives of those He calls! This man became a warrior for the gospel, establishing churches, and growing disciples. As a result he repeatedly endured extensive persecution.

2. Who is Timothy? Read Acts 16:1–5 to learn about this partner in the gospel.

	Where was Timothy from?

	What do you learn about his parents? (See 2 Tim. 1:5 to learn the names of his grandmother and mother.)

What was his reputation?

Timothy became a "soul-son" to Paul, traveling with him on his second and third missionary journeys. These two men of God developed such a close bond that Paul later wrote two personal letters (1–2 Timothy) to his friend that were included in the canon of Scripture.

3. As he begins this letter, the author identifies himself not as an apostle but as a _____

4. WORD STUDY: servant (1:1)
   Greek word (Strong's #1401):

   Definition:

Paul is physically chained to a Roman guard as he writes this letter (you will look into the back story of this in upcoming lessons), and yet he identifies himself as a slave of Christ Jesus. Paul makes clear that his devotion and allegiance are not to a city or a governing authority but to the reigning and ruling Master. It is truly paradoxical that through humble service one will find true freedom.

5. To whom was this book written?

6. Of whom does Paul make special mention in this verse?

Overseers are also known as elders. They shepherd the people of God. They are called to exude spiritual maturity and give spiritual oversight within the life of the church. Deacons are also known as ministers or servants. They serve the people of God. They are called to exude spiritual benevolence and spiritual practicality as they meet physical needs and minister within the church.

7. Background: city of Philippi

    Read Acts 16:12 and write down what you learn about the city of Philippi.

8. Background: Philippian church

    The church at Philippi was likely established about A.D. 50 when Paul visited the first time. There was only a small Jewish population in this city, not even a group large enough to warrant a formal place of worship. The church was made up of mostly Gentile believers, therefore Paul does not quote the Old Testament in this letter as he does in other writings.

    Read Acts 16:13. Who was gathered and what was their purpose for gathering?

    Read Acts 16:14–15. Who was this church's first convert and what do you learn about her?

    Read Acts 16:16–40. What other significant things happened on this trip and to whom?

9. Which of the following literary genres best describes the book of Philippians?
    _____ narrative
    _____ poem
    _____ letter

_____ prophetic

_____ apocalyptic

Philippians is known as a "prison epistle" since it was written while Paul was in chains for the gospel. As you will see, Philippians is a personal letter (as opposed to a circular letter that was delivered to several churches throughout a given region). It was written to a body of believers for whom Paul has deep affection, and likely delivered to the Philippian church by a man named Epaphroditus, whom we will learn more about as we study. Like all New Testament letters, Philippians was meant to be read aloud to its recipients. These letters were Paul's way of staying connected to the churches he helped establish and his continued work of discipleship in their lives.

10. Based on what you've learned so far, approximately when was this book written?

_____ before Paul's missionary journeys

_____ during Paul's missionary journeys

_____ after Paul's missionary journeys

There are varying opinions on exactly where Paul was living when he wrote this letter. He was undoubtedly under house arrest, and while some believe Paul may have written from either Ephesus or Caesarea, most theologians believe Paul was in the city of Rome at the time of this writing. It's likely that Paul dictated this letter to his friend Timothy, who penned the message on paper for the Philippian church about ten years after the church was established at Philippi, putting its date between A.D. 59-61 (several years after completing his missionary journeys).

11. What do you know about why this book was written?

Paul had several reasons for writing: to thank the church for their gift and ongoing support; to give updates on himself, Timothy, and Epaphroditus (all of whom the Philippians would know); to encourage the church in the joy of the Lord; and to urge them toward Christlikeness as they grow to know the immeasurable worth of Jesus. Themes of encouragement, joy, humility, unity, and steadfastness are evident throughout the body of this letter. Paul writes to awaken the hearts and revive the souls of the Philippian believers in the absolute treasure of Christ.

PAUL'S GREETING TO THE CHURCH
"Grace and peace from God our Father and the Lord Jesus Christ." (1:2)

This was a typical greeting for the time and culture but be sure not to overlook its significance. These opening words embody key elements of the Christian life.

12. WORD STUDY: grace (1:2)
    Greek word (Strong's #5485):

    Definition:

13. WORD STUDY: peace (1:2)
    Greek word (Strong's #1515):

    Definition:

Grace is a simple summary of the gospel. Understanding the merciful kindness and undeserved favor of God inevitably results in the confident assurance of salvation. Grace is the root of the Christian life. Peace is the fruit that naturally follows. Paul longs for the Philippian church to experience deeper levels of this grace and peace, making a point to offer this initial greeting to the Philippian church in both the name of God the Father and the Lord Jesus Christ.

NOTES

"Revive us again,
Fill each heart with Thy love;
May each soul be rekindled
With fire from above.
Hallelujah! Thine the glory,
Hallelujah! Amen;
Hallelujah! Thine the glory;
Revive us again."

"Revive Us Again" [2]

Week Two

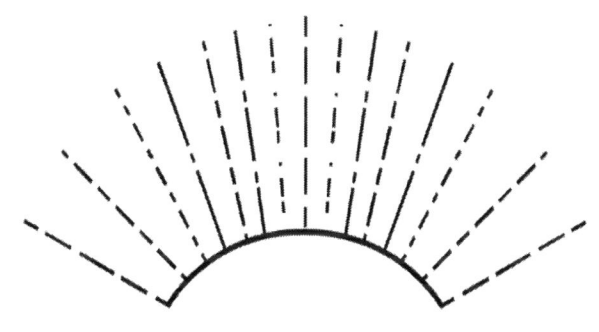

**AWAKEN
TO
THE FELLOWSHIP OF CHRIST**

Philippians 1:3–11

DAY ONE
TAKE IT IN
1. Read through the book of Philippians.
2. Read Philippians 1:3–11 in the English Standard Version (ESV).

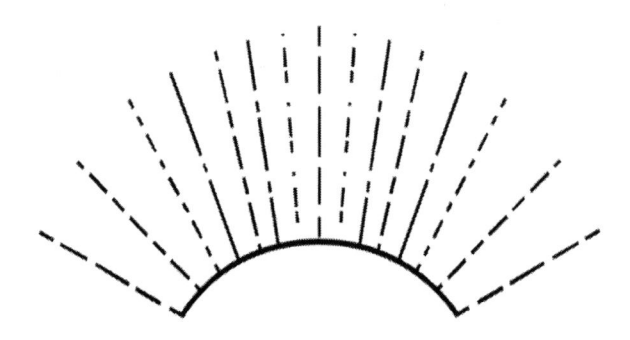

WRITE IT DOWN
3. Write down any initial thoughts, responses, and/or questions.

4. Highlight the following words in the ESV text:
   Pray/prayer – PURPLE circle
   Joy/Rejoice – YELLOW highlight
   Gospel – ORANGE highlight
   Christ – YELLOW circle

5. Write out this week's memory verse: Philippians 1:6 ESV. Write it down, study it, post it around your house. Make it a goal to memorize it this week.

DAY TWO
THINK IT THROUGH AND STORE IT UP
Focus on Philippians 1:3–6 ESV as you complete the following:

1. Paul is writing from prison, yet who is his focus as he begins this letter?

2. Review Acts 16:14–18, 25–34. Who specifically might Paul be calling to mind as he begins writing? Describe the people who were the first members of this church. What does this tell you about God and the people of His church?

3. What attitude does Paul demonstrate as he writes his letter to the church in Philippi?

4. Today's passage includes Paul's first mention of one of the main themes of this letter.

   WORD STUDY: joy (1:4)
   Greek word (Strong's #5479):

   Definition:

5. What is "partnership in the gospel"?

6. WORD STUDY: partnership (1:5)
   Greek word (Strong's #2842):

   Definition:

7. When did this partnership begin? How long will it last?

8. What is the "good work" that was begun in the lives of the Philippian believers?

9. When will this work be complete and who will see to it that it is accomplished?

10. What is "the day of Jesus Christ"? (See also 2 Cor. 5:10, and 1 Thes. 5:2.) What will happen on that day? (See Rom. 2:5–6 and Heb. 9:27–28.)

MAKE IT COUNT

11. The gratefulness, confidence, and joy with which Paul prays for this body of believers demonstrates his deep personal affections for them. How would you describe your prayers for the community of believers to which you belong? Do you find deep gratefulness and abiding joy when you pray for them? Write a note and send it to a close Christian friend, letting them know how thankful you are for his/her friendship and partnership in the gospel.

12. Has God started the good work of salvation in you? Do you believe He will be faithful to complete it? What does that mean to you?

13. The Greek word for "partnership" means fellowship. Believers can only be partners in the gospel if we are first in fellowship with Christ. How does your fellowship with Christ awaken your life and revive your soul? Explain how this then creates opportunity for gospel partnerships with other believers.

DAY THREE
TAKE IT IN
1. Read Philippians 1:3–11 in the Amplified Version (AMP).

WRITE IT DOWN
2. This week's memory verse is Philippians 1:6 ESV. Fill in the blanks: And I am _____ of this, that _____ who began a good _____ in you will _____ it to _____ at the day of _____ Christ.

THINK IT THROUGH AND STORE IT UP
Focus on Philippians 1:7–8 ESV.

In Acts 16, we saw God take three people of different ages, genders, backgrounds, and life experiences and grab hold of each one by the power of the gospel. He united this motley crew of misfits and grew them into the body of believers to whom Paul now writes. We can sense the revival in his own soul as he remembers his time with them. Paul wants to also revive their souls as he points them to the fullness of God in Christ.

3. Paul writes, "It is right for me to feel this way about you." What does this indicate is the proper connection and affection we should have for other believers? John 13:35 says, "By this all people will know that you are my disciples, if you . . . " If you do what?

4. Re-read Philippians 1:3–8 and circle the word *all* every time you see it. This indicates a sense of impartiality and unity, a quality Jesus Himself prays for those who follow Him (see John 17).

5. WORD STUDY: partakers (1:7)
   Greek word (Strong's #4791):

   Definition:

   What word is this similar to? Why is that important?

6. How (in what situations) does Paul say the Philippian believers are partakers of grace?

   The fact that the believers associate with Paul even in prison is a testimony to Paul's impact in their lives and their ongoing devotion to and fellowship with Christ.

7. Paul yearns (earnestly desires, longs for) these believers. This kind of spiritual connection is the result of true fellowship with Christ. Read Psalm 63:1-8. What are the actions and reactions of one who longs for God?

8. God's love drew Paul into fellowship with Christ. Paul then grew in love and compassion toward others, especially those with whom he ministered and established churches. Paul had an outstanding and deeply personal connection to the church in Philippi.

WORD STUDY: affection (1:8)
Greek word (Strong's #4698):

Definition:

9. Who/what is the basis of Paul's affection?

10. Paul exemplifies here what he wrote in Romans 12:10. Write it below.

Affection is deeper than personal feelings or fleeting passions. Affection involves the seat of the emotions, the core of one's being. In today's world we refer to the heart as the center from which our affections flow ("I love you with all my heart"). In the first century church, however, the seat of the emotions was the bowels, or the sum of one's inward parts, which would require a very different phrase. But regardless of the cultural expressions used to communicate love and joy, our connection to Christ inevitably impacts the relationships we establish and grow with His people. When we are in fellowship with Christ and with other believers we begin to love them the way Jesus loves us.

MAKE IT COUNT

11. Are you consumed by God and a desire to fellowship with Him? Can you honestly say, "God, I've *got* to have You?" Does your heart yearn for Him? Write down or pray aloud the prayer of David in Psalm 63:1–8.

12. With whom are you a partaker of grace? Describe your relationships with these people.

13. In what practical ways can you come alongside a pastor, missionary, or friend in defending and confirming the truth of the gospel? Commit to following through on at least one of those ways this week.

DAY FOUR
TAKE IT IN
1. Read Philippians 1:3–11 in the New Living Translation (NLT).

WRITE IT DOWN
2. Fill in the blanks for this week's memory verse: Philippians 1:6 ESV.
   And _____ am _____ of _____, that _____ who _____ a _____ work in _____ will _____ it to _____at the _____ of _____ _____.

THINK IT THROUGH AND STORE IT UP

Focus on Philippians 1:9–11 ESV.

3. What is Paul's first prayerful desire for these believers? Why might he have started with this? (See 1 Cor. 13:13 and Col. 3:14.)

4. WORD STUDY: abound (1:9)
   Greek word (Strong's #4052):

   Definition:

5. What should this abounding love include?

6. For what reason should abounding love include these things? (so that...)

Christians should never stop learning and growing in love and spiritual maturity. Abounding love deepens and matures as we awaken to the treasure of Christ. Love that abounds more and more links the head (knowledge) with the heart (discernment) of a Christ-follower. This depth of insight is more than simply gaining information; it also includes a practical application of knowledge and a godly perception for the best way to do so. Abounding love leads to abundant life.

7. WORD STUDY: approve (1:10)
   Greek word (Strong's #1381):

   Definition:

8. What does it mean to be pure and blameless as we live each day? How does approving what is excellent lead to this outcome?

"As Christians, often the most difficult challenge we face is not in distinguishing between good and evil. Rather the most challenging choices are often in deciding between what is good, better and best in how to love others."[3] Approving what is excellent enables us to love others in the best possible ways.

9. Abounding love also leads to a life filled with "the fruit of righteousness." What do you learn about the fruit of righteousness in Philippians 1:11 NLT and Hebrews 12:11? What specific qualities might this include? (See Gal. 5:22–23 and Col. 3:12–17.)

10. What is the result of this kind of living, which should always be our greatest passion (Phil. 1:11)?

MAKE IT COUNT

11. Do you have someone like Paul in your life who earnestly and fervently prays for your fellowship with Christ and integrity of character? If yes, who? If not, who could be this person for you?

12. For whom are you praying the prayer of Philippians 1:9–11? Who might God be calling you to mentor/disciple?

13. Are you abounding in love more and more, with knowledge and discernment? Are you filled with the fruit of righteousness? Give examples of what this looks like in your life. What are some ways you can bear more fruit?

14. Write out Philippians 1:6 ESV from memory.

PRAYING WITH JOY

Lord Jesus,

As I work through this study of Philippians, I pray with joy, thanking you for the treasure of your Word and for calling me into deeper fellowship with Christ. I am a servant and gospel partner, longing to share the transforming message of the gospel wherever you would have me go. Thank you for the good work you have undoubtedly begun in me. I am confident you will continue this work in me until it is complete.

As a partaker of grace, I don't want to be content to only know the gospel but be committed to sharing it with others. Fill my heart with passion to jointly participate in kingdom initiatives, working with an "energetic wholeheartedness"[4] that captivates the world. God, cause your love to abound in and through me; compel me to pursue greater knowledge and understanding of eternal things. Please grant wisdom and discernment, so I can recognize how to best love and serve others in every situation.

God, I long to run with endurance, daily confessing sin, and relying on you to purify my heart. Please fill my life with evidence that you are at work within me. Cause my life to bear fruit, so that others can see the light and love and joy of Jesus. Grant grace to live every moment to the praise and glory of Christ alone, for this is a life of abundance and joy!

Awaken my heart and revive my soul as I live in the grace of the Lord Jesus Christ, the love of God, and the fellowship of the Holy Spirit (2 Cor. 13:14). I love you, Lord, and want to know you as my greatest treasure.

For your glory alone,

Amen.

AWAKEN

NOTES

"Then in fellowship sweet
We will sit at His feet,
Or we'll walk by His side in the way;
What He says we will do
Where He sends we will go –
Never fear, only trust and obey."

"Trust and Obey"[5]

Week Three

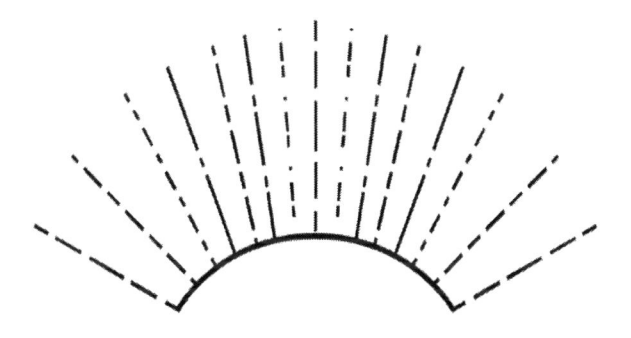

**AWAKEN
TO
THE SATISFACTION OF CHRIST**

Philippians 1:12–30

DAY ONE
TAKE IT IN
1. Read through the book of Philippians.
2. Read Philippians 1:12–30 ESV.

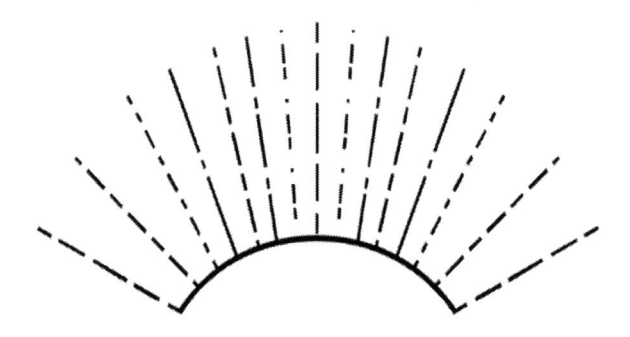

WRITE IT DOWN
3. Write down any initial thoughts, responses, and/or questions.

4. Highlight each of these recurring words in the ESV:
   Gospel – ORANGE highlight
   Christ – YELLOW circle
   Joy/Rejoice – YELLOW highlight
   Live/Life – PURPLE rectangle
   Prayer – PURPLE circle

5. Write out this week's memory verse: Philippians 1:20–21 ESV. Write it down, study it, post it around your house. Make it a goal to memorize it this week.

DAY TWO
THINK IT THROUGH AND STORE IT UP

Focus on Philippians 1:12–18 ESV as you complete the following.

1. Paul's shifts his focus from the Philippian church to whom/what?

2. Read 1:12 in the NLT. What is "everything that has happened?"
   The full story begins in Acts 21:27. The remaining chapters of Acts detail all that Paul has already endured. Skim those chapters and note your findings below.

3. How could these things have derailed and discouraged Paul?

4. How have Paul's circumstances served to advance the gospel?

   Paul demonstrates unwavering faith in the plan and sovereignty of God. Paul saw even his imprisonment as a blessing; a unique opportunity to share Christ with a group of people who may not have otherwise heard it. "For *everyone* here, including the *whole* palace guard, knows that I am in chains because of Christ" (Phil. 1:13 NLT, emphasis mine). Paul may have been in chains, but the Word of God was not.

5. What has happened to other believers as a result? Why might they have responded a different way?

6. What are the opposing reasons people are preaching the gospel and with what motives?

7. Are these false teachers (are they distorting the gospel message)? How do you know? Compare Philippians 1:15 with 2 Corinthians 11:4. What difference do you notice about the message being preached?

8. What does Philippians 1:16 reveal about Paul's belief in the sovereignty of God?

9. What is Paul's attitude toward those trying to afflict him?

10. In what does Paul find satisfaction and rejoice?

Paul experiences joy despite his circumstances because his eyes remain fixed on Jesus and the advancement of the gospel. Other preachers were out to cause him harm, yet he could still respond with joy because "what matters is the content of the preaching, not the identity of the preacher."[6] Paul knew God could take what the enemy meant for evil and turn it for good. God can and will use anyone He chooses to fulfill His plan and make Himself known.

MAKE IT COUNT

11. What unplanned or difficult circumstances in your life opened unexpected doors of gospel opportunity? Did you make the most of that opportunity? If yes, how so? If not, how has this lesson awakened you to respond differently next time?

12. One awakened believer with a contagious passion for God has the potential to inspire countless others to change the world for Christ. Recall and share a time when someone else's unwavering faith and joy in the midst of difficulty bolstered your gospel courage.

13. How are you awakening to the satisfaction of Christ? In what ways is His ultimate satisfaction reviving your soul? What impact is it having on others?

DAY THREE
TAKE IT IN
1. Read Philippians 1:12–30 AMP.

WRITE IT DOWN

2. This week's memory verse is Philippians 1:20–21 ESV. Fill in the blanks:

   As it is my _____ expectation and _____ that I will not be at all _____, but that with full _____ now as _____ Christ will be _____ in my body, whether by _____ or by _____. For to me to _____ is Christ, and to die is _____.

THINK IT THROUGH AND STORE IT UP

Focus on Philippians 1:19–26 ESV.

The Philippians are deeply concerned for Paul, the man who had established their church and who had become their friend and brother in Christ. Paul shares the state of his heart despite the uncertainty of his future. He reassures them that no matter what happens, Christ will be exalted and God glorified.

3. For what reason does Paul rejoice?

4. WORD STUDY: deliverance (1:19)
   Greek word (Strong's #4991):

   Definition:

5. Paul's deliverance could mean being delivered from his chains or being delivered to his Christ. Why would either one be cause for Paul to rejoice?

6. What is the eager expectation and hope of Paul?

7. The original language of 1:21 does not include the word *is* and therefore reads like this: "For me to live Christ and to die gain." What does he mean? (See also Jn. 11:26; 2 Cor. 5:8; Col. 3:4.)

8. WORD STUDY: live (1:21)
   Greek word (Strong's #2198):

   Definition:

   In John 10:10, Jesus said He came to bring *zōē*, which means "abundant fullness of life." The Greek root word for *zōē* is the same word Paul uses here for *live*. He undoubtedly experienced abundant fullness of life as a result of deep satisfaction in Christ.

9. "To live is Christ and to die is gain." Which option does Paul determine is "far better"? Which option does Paul consider "more necessary" and for whom?

10. Paul exudes confidence that he will be released. How does he intend to use his freedom?

    "What is your only comfort in life and in death?
    That I am not my own, but I belong – body and soul, in life and in death –
    to my faithful Savior Jesus Christ."[7]

MAKE IT COUNT

11. The eager expectation mentioned in Philippians 1:20 indicates stretching one's neck forward, straining to see what's coming. Can you relate to Paul's eager expectation and hope? Are you confident Christ will be honored both in your life and in your death? If not, spend time in prayer about this. If yes, do your best to put that confidence into words in the space below.

12. Did you know it is possible to be alive yet not truly live? How are you truly experiencing *zōē* (abundant fullness of life)? If you do not yet enjoy abundant fullness of life, what changes do you need to make in order to do so?

13. Are you so in love with Jesus that you view death as gain? Explain your answer.

DAY FOUR
TAKE IT IN
1. Read Philippians 1:12–30 NLT.

WRITE IT DOWN
2. Fill in the blanks for this week's memory verse: Philippians 1:20–21 ESV.

As _____ is my _____ _____ and hope that _____ will _____ be at all _____, but that with _____ _____ now as always _____will be _____in my _____, whether by _____ or by _____. For to _____ to _____ is _____and to _____ is _____.

THINK IT THROUGH AND STORE IT UP
Focus on Philippians 1:27–30 ESV.

3. If we belong to Christ, this world is not our home. We are only strangers passing through. As such, how are believers to live, according to 1:27? What does this mean? (See also Eph. 4:1–3 and Col. 1:10.)

4. Based on Philippians 1:27, what word or two describes Paul's desire for the church regardless of where he is?

5. WORD STUDY: standing firm (1:27)
Greek word (Strong's #4739):

Definition:

6. With what attitude are the people to stand firm? List three phrases Paul uses in 1:27–28 to describe this.

7. Who are the opponents Paul mentions in 1:28? (See also Phil. 3:2 and Gal. 1:8-9.) Notice these are not the same as those preaching Christ insincerely in Philippians 1:15–17.

8. What two imminent results will a fearless stance indicate to their enemies?

9. What two privileges come to those who identify with Christ (see 1:29 NLT)?

Christ endured suffering on this earth. Those who follow Him should expect nothing less, even counting suffering a privilege. While we don't like or enjoy it, we can find joy in the hard things, confident that suffering will lead to glory. The unbelieving world notices how believers endure trials and suffering of various kinds. It's up to us to ensure they see Christ magnified in our responses; our goal is to show them the bigness of our God in the messiness of this earth.

10. Paul writes this letter to the church body. He tells them to live worthy, stand firm, strive side by side, demonstrate gospel courage . . . together with one mind and spirit. When suffering comes (and it will), these are the people who will endure . . . together. How is this an encouragement? How does this result in joy?

MAKE IT COUNT

11. Are you living a worthy life? How is your life magnifying the gospel and glorifying God?

12. "Fearless faith results from holding on to Christ as our treasure [and ultimate satisfaction]. Gospel courage comes from gospel preciousness."[8] Would you describe the gospel as absolutely precious to you? Write out a prayer for fearless faith and gospel courage.

13. "For you have been given not only the privilege of trusting in Christ but also the privilege of suffering for him. We are in this struggle together" (Phil. 1:29–30 NLT). We don't often view both trusting and suffering as privileges. Describe your experience of trusting in Christ. Describe your experience of suffering for Christ. How does this impact you to know that in neither experience are you alone?

14. Write out Philippians 1:20–21 ESV from memory.

> "All who come to Christ with reverent humility and godly fear will receive infinite satisfaction, blessings upon blessings…grace upon grace."

PRAYING WITH JOY

Heavenly Father,

Because you are sovereign, I can rest knowing that all my life circumstances are a part of a bigger picture, one that is all about your purpose. So I pray for joy even in difficulty because I trust you are mighty to save and will undoubtedly use all things for my good by the power of your Spirit and for your glory.

Lord, use my faith in hard circumstances to embolden others in their faith, opening doors of unique gospel opportunity. Help me always to preach Christ with a pure heart; not to make a name for myself, but to make you famous. Give me faith and humility to know you will use whomever you please (Christ-follower or not) to advance and fulfill your plan. Let that not frustrate me, but cause joy to abound in knowing you will be glorified!

Lord, I long to live with eager expectation and hope. Give me full courage without an ounce of shame to believe you will be honored in me, no matter what happens—life or death. To be alive here on the earth means I get to live a life all about you—knowing you, preaching you, sharing you, and glorifying you. When death comes, I get to be in your presence experiencing fullness of joy in the glories of heaven. It's a win-win for me. Fill me with desire, energy, and passion to fulfill your purpose for me; to disciple others that they may also have joy in their faith. Make my life an example, an influence that will bring joy to others and glory to you.

Be magnified in me Jesus, so my life is worthy of the gospel of Christ. You are my all in all, and I praise you, O God. Satisfy me in the morning with your steadfast love, that I may rejoice and be glad all my days (Ps. 90:14). Awaken my heart and revive my soul in the treasure that you are.

In Jesus' Name,

Amen.

NOTES

"Praise to the Lord!
O let all that is in me adore him!
All that hath life and breath,
Come now with praises before him!
Let the Amen
Sound from his people again:
Gladly for aye we adore him."

"Praise to the Lord, the Almighty"[9]

Week Four

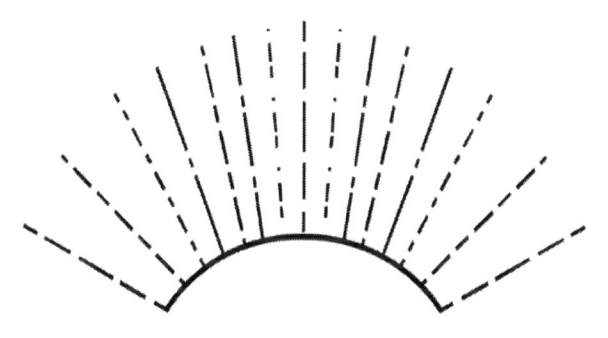

AWAKEN
TO
THE MIND OF CHRIST

Philippians 2:1–11

DAY ONE
TAKE IT IN

1. Read through the book of Philippians.
2. Read Philippians 2:1–11 ESV.

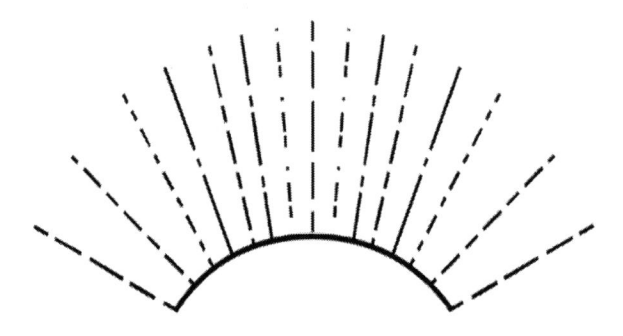

   WRITE IT DOWN
3. Write down any initial thoughts, responses, and/or questions.

4. Highlight each of these recurring words in the ESV:
   Joy – YELLOW highlight
   Christ/Jesus – YELLOW circle
   Humility/humbled – GREEN underline

5. Write out this week's memory verse: Philippians 2:1–2 ESV. Write it down, study it, post it around your house. Make it a goal to memorize it this week.

DAY TWO
THINK IT THROUGH AND STORE IT UP.

Focus on Philippians 2:1-4 ESV as you complete the following.

Before Paul addresses a specific situation happening within the church (mentioned in Phil. 4), he expresses his intense desire for the church collectively—solidarity within the body. Above his concern regarding his own release, Paul shows concern for the spiritual progress of the church.

1. In Philippians 2:1 Paul uses the word "so," or "therefore" to link his thoughts from 1:27 to what he is about to say in 2:1-4. What key theme/idea is he repeating?

2. "Because" or "since" could replace "if" as Paul begins 2:1. What four realities of being in Christ does Paul mention in this verse? List them below.

3. What does Paul ask the Philippians to do as a result of those four realities?

4. How are the believers to accomplish this according to 2:2?

5. With what attitude should we live?

6. WORD STUDY: humility (2:3)
   Greek word (Strong's #5012):

   Definition:

7. What is the opposite of humility? What are two ways this is manifested (see 2:3)?

8. Humility was not a highly esteemed virtue in the Greek culture of the day. It was considered a low value, of little dignity, indicating failure or shame. "The concept was entirely foreign to the Greek and utterly abhorrent to the Romans."[10]

   Look up the following verses and write down how God views and responds to humility:

   Proverbs 3:34 -

   Matthew 23:12 -

   Luke 18:14 -

   James 4:6, 10 -

   1 Peter 5:5–6 -

9. How should we view others according to this passage of Philippians? Does this mean we neglect ourselves? How do you know? (See Phil. 2:4 and Matt. 22:39.)

10. What does it mean to look to the interests of others? (See also Rom. 15:1–2 and Gal. 6:2.)

MAKE IT COUNT

11. Look at the four realities you listed in your answer to question 2. How are each of these realities demonstrated in your daily living? How does your life prove the gospel is true?

12. Selfish ambition is motivated by desire to gain. Conceit is motivated by desire to gloat. In what areas are you living with hopes to gain? In what areas are you living with desire to gloat? Ask God to search your heart and confess any offensive ways He reveals to you.

13. What is one thing you can do this week to take an interest in others over yourself?

DAY THREE
TAKE IT IN
1. Read Philippians 2:1–11 AMP.

WRITE IT DOWN
2. This week's memory verse is Philippians 2:1–2 ESV. Fill in the blanks:
So if there is any _____ in Christ, any _____ from love, any _____ in the Spirit, any _____ and sympathy, complete my _____ by being of the same _____, having the same _____, being in full _____ and of one _____.

THINK IT THROUGH AND STORE IT UP
Focus on Philippians 2:5–8 ESV.

These verses mark the beginning of what is often known as an early hymn of the church.

3. What does Paul say in 2:5 "is yours in Christ Jesus"?

4. List all the characteristics given in these verses that describe the mind and life of Christ.

5. Write out 2:6 from the Amplified Version. How does this help you better understand who Jesus is? (See also Col. 1:19.)

6. WORD STUDY: emptied (2:7)
   Greek Word (Strong's #2758):

   Definition:

   Write out Paul's description of "emptied" from 1 Corinthians 9:15.

7. Based on what you know about who Jesus is, of what did He empty Himself? Of what did Jesus NOT empty Himself? (This is important!)

   Jesus was both fully God and fully man. To take on human form means Jesus grew tired and needed physical rest. He needed daily food and drink. He needed social interaction. Jesus felt joy and sorrow, pain, temptation, and suffering. To remain fully divine means even in His humanity, Jesus never sinned. It also means He never relinquished His rights and privileges as God, but Jesus chose not to exercise His deity for His own advantage. While never voiding Himself of His divine power, Jesus surrendered His will in complete obedience to the Father.

8. Read Matthew 20:28. Give examples from the ministry of Jesus that show Him to be a servant (check out the following gospel stories if you need some help with this: Matt.12:15–21; Mk. 1:29-34; Lk. 9:10–17; Jn. 13:1–20).

9. What was the purpose of His obedience and death? (See also Gal. 4:4–5 and Eph. 5:25–27.)

10. What was significant about death by crucifixion? (See Deut. 21:23 and Gal. 3:13.)

Modern-day believers view the cross as a sacred symbol, often adorning ourselves, our homes, and our churches with variations of it. But in the New Testament Greco-Roman world, people would not speak of "the cross" as it was considered an obscenity. Crucifixion in biblical times was reserved for the worst of criminals, and even the thought of the cross provoked unspeakable horror and disgust. Once the sign of horrific death, the cross is now the boast of eternal life.

MAKE IT COUNT

11. Jesus willfully lived and died in obedience to the Father. He could have chosen to do none of it but decided to endure all of it.[11] Jesus made this decision…with you in mind. What is your response to all He's done for you?

12. Humility involves both service and sacrifice. How are you humbly serving those around you? What are you sacrificing for the sake of Christ and others?

13. In what ways have you awakened to the mind of Christ? How does sharing the attitude of Jesus bring revival to your soul?

DAY FOUR
TAKE IT IN
1. Read Philippians 2:1–11 NLT.

WRITE IT DOWN
2. Fill in the blanks for this week's memory verse: Philippians 2:1–2 ESV.
So if there is any _____ in _____, any _____ from _____, any _____ in the _____, any _____ and _____, complete my _____ by being of the _____ mind, having the _____ love, being in _____ accord and of _____ mind.

THINK IT THROUGH AND STORE IT UP
Focus on Philippians 2:9–11 ESV.

3. What is the "therefore" there for? For what reason has God done what Paul explains in these verses?

4. WORD STUDY: exalted (2:9)
Greek Word (Strong's #5251):

Definition:

5. Jesus' obedience and suffering leads to His exaltation. All He had set aside to fulfill God's redemptive plan would be restored to Him completely. The exaltation of Christ includes several events following His crucifixion. Note the progression below:

   Matthew 28:5–6 -

   Luke 24:50–51 -

   Hebrews 1:3 -

   Colossians 1:16–17 -

   Revelation 11:15 -

6. What is the name the Father has graciously granted to the Son in 2:9–11?

   WORD STUDY: Lord (2:11)
   Greek Word (Strong's #2962)

   Definition:

7. What does it mean that His name is "above every name"?
   (See also 1 Chron.17:20; Is. 40:25; Rev. 19:16.)

8. How will all people one day respond to Jesus?

9. How can this happen if not everyone believes?

10. What is the purpose and final result of Christ's exaltation?

> "And there is no other god besides me,
> a righteous God and a Savior;
> there is none besides me.
>
> Turn to me and be saved,
> all the ends of the earth!
> For I am God, and there is no other.
> By myself I have sworn;
> from my mouth has gone out in righteousness
> a word that shall not return:
> 'To me every knee shall bow,
> every tongue shall swear allegiance'" (Is. 45:21-23).

Whether in faith or in judgment, one day every person in all of history will acknowledge Jesus Christ as Lord, and God will be glorified.

MAKE IT COUNT

11. What is the difference between confessing the lordship of Jesus Christ and surrendering to the lordship of Jesus Christ? Have you both confessed and surrendered to His lordship?

12. Spend some time in worship, singing songs that lift the name of Jesus and celebrate Jesus Christ as Lord. Write down some of the lyrics that are most powerful to you and why.

13. Reread the following verses: Proverbs 29:23; James 4:10; 1 Peter 5:5–6.
    These were true even of Jesus. How are these verses an encouragement to you?

14. Write out Philippians 2:1–2 ESV from memory.

PRAYING WITH JOY

Oh Jesus,

Yours is the sweetest name I know. You are my greatest source of encouragement. Your love brings me comfort. Your Spirit is alive and working within me. God, I seek to honor you by sharing the mind of Christ and by being filled with the love of Christ, living in unity with my brothers and sisters in Christ. Bring about fullness of joy in my life. Help me to live selflessly, not doing things to gain or gloat. Give me grace to exude humility, putting others ahead of myself. Give me a heart that is genuinely concerned for others. God, humble me to follow the example of Christ, who was willing to give up the glories of heaven and set aside His divine privileges to walk among those He came to save here on this earth.

Lord, grant faith so strong that I will follow you in willing obedience, even if it means my death. Help me to remember that the last will be first, and the humble will one day be exalted. Lord Jesus, your name is above every other name. I surrender myself to you. Your name will be praised, for you alone are God. One day everyone will know it and bow down before you, boldly declaring that Jesus Christ is Lord, and God the Father will finally receive all the glory due His name!

As I seek to know you as my greatest treasure, I pray that I will love you, Lord God, with all my heart and with all my soul and with all my mind (Matt. 22:37).

Christ alone be praised!

Amen.

NOTES

"May the mind of Christ my Savior
Live in me from day to day,
By his love and pow'r controlling
All I do and say."

"May the Mind of Christ My Savior"[12]

Week Five

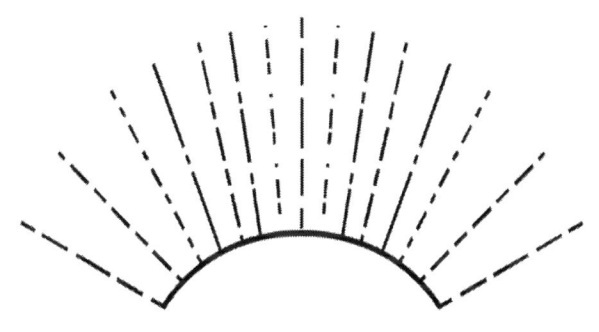

AWAKEN
TO
THE WORK OF CHRIST

Philippians 2:12–30

DAY ONE
TAKE IT IN
1. Read through the book of Philippians.
2. Read Philippians 2:12–30 NLT.

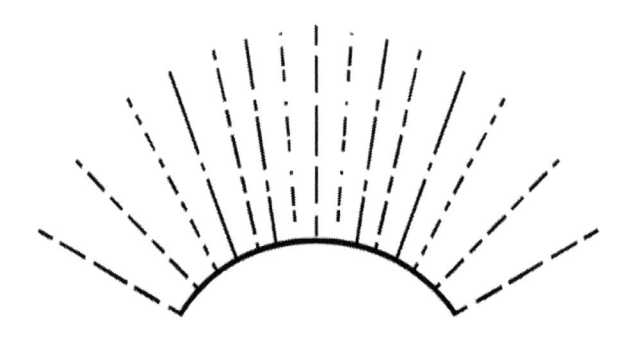

WRITE IT DOWN
3. Write down any initial thoughts, responses, and/or questions.

4. Highlight each of these recurring words in the ESV:
   Joy/Rejoice – YELLOW highlight
   Christ – YELLOW circle
   Gospel – ORANGE highlight
   Life – PURPLE rectangle
   Work – RED underline

5. Write out this week's memory verse: Philippians 2:12b–13 ESV. Write it down, study it, post it around your house. Make it a goal to memorize it this week.

DAY TWO
THINK IT THROUGH AND STORE IT UP

Focus on Philippians 2:12–18 ESV as you complete the following.

Paul begins this section with "therefore," linking this passage to what he has previously stated. He has clearly portrayed the humble obedience of Christ (2:6–11) and now urges the church to follow His example in their continued pursuit of holiness.

1. What word does Paul use to address his readers, and what two things does this continue to indicate?

2. What does it mean to "work out your salvation with fear and trembling"? How is this different from working to earn your salvation? Explain what kind of fear this involves (see 2:12 AMP).

3. Who is working in the lives of believers? What does this work compel believers to do? What does this look like in real life?

The English word *energy* comes from the Greek word used here for *work*. God initiates the work and then energizes, equips, and empowers believers to accomplish the work of Christ in the world.

4. How does Paul command the church to live?
   vs. 14 Do _____
   vs. 15 Be _____
   vs. 15 Shine _____
   vs. 16 Hold _____

5. The Philippian church is not the only group of believers who faced these issues and needed these reminders. What did the Israelites say and do in Numbers 14:1–4 and 20:2–5? How does Moses refer to them in Deuteronomy 32:5, 20? What can we learn from this?

6. To be blameless and innocent means to be free from fault or offense, above reproach, and not troubled by the consciousness of sin. How does this relate to Paul's words about grumbling and complaining in Philippians 2:14?

7. Reread Philippians 2:15. What two phrases indicate how believers are called to pursue holiness? Ponder this and note your thoughts.

8. WORD STUDY: lights (2:15)
   Greek Word (Strong's # 5458):

Definition:

To hold fast also means "to hold forth." What must we cling tightly to ourselves while simultaneously extending to others in order to shine as lights in the world?

Read Psalm 56:13, Matthew 5:14, John 8:12, and Ephesians 5:8 and write down the connection you find between light and life.

9. The Old Testament sacrificial system included a drink offering (see Ex. 29:38–41), but these sacrifices are no longer needed because they have been fulfilled in the person and work of Jesus Christ. Knowing this, read what Paul writes in Romans 12:1 regarding sacrifice. What then does Paul mean in today's passage by being "poured out as a drink offering"?

10. What attitude does Paul exude as well as exhort in 2:18, and why can this be a reality in the life of believers?

MAKE IT COUNT

We are called to join God in the work He is doing in our personal lives, our families, our churches, and our communities. Being called by God doesn't give us excuse to be lazy or lukewarm in our faith. We don't simply "let go and let

God," essentially absolving ourselves from any responsibility for our own spiritual growth. We cooperate with the work of the Spirit to ensure that the church maintains red hot faith!

11. Explain what it looks like in your life to work out your salvation with fear and trembling.

12. How well are you obeying the commands Paul issues in 2:14–16 (review question 4)? Be specific in your answers.

13. Paul tells believers to shine against the darkness of the world; not to remove ourselves from the world but to make a difference from within. In what ways are you pursuing holiness and practicing godliness right here in the midst of a crooked and twisted generation? How are you illuminating the truth of the gospel among those with whom you live, work, worship, and play?

DAY THREE
TAKE IT IN
1. Read Philippians 2:12–30 ESV.

WRITE IT DOWN

2. This week's memory verse is Philippians 2:12b–13 ESV. Fill in the blanks:

_____ out your own _____ with fear and _____, for it is _____ who _____ in you both to _____ and to _____ for his good _____.

THINK IT THROUGH AND STORE IT UP
Focus on Philippians 2:19–24 ESV.

Paul devotes time in the remaining verses of chapter two to commend two men who are partners with him in the gospel; two "ordinary saints"[13] with whom the church at Philippi has history and holds in high regard; two men who exemplify the mind of Christ as they do the work of Christ.

3. Who does Paul hope to send to Philippi and for what reason?

4. WORD STUDY: like him (2:20)
   Literal translation:

   Greek Word (Strong's # 2473):

   Definition:

   The soul-connection between Paul and Timothy demonstrates exactly the joyful unity and kindred spirit Paul urges of the Philippian church.

5. WORD STUDY: be concerned (2:20)
   Greek Word (Strong's #3309):

   Definition:

   This can be negative or positive. Which is it here?

6. Who are the "they" Paul mentions in 2:21? (See Phil.1:15–17 and 2:21 AMP for possibilities.)

7. How has Timothy proven his character? (See Acts 16:1–5; 17:14–15; 1 Cor. 4:14–17.) Why is this important?

8. To what does Paul liken his relationship to Timothy in Philippians 4:22?

9. When does Paul plan to send Timothy to the Philippian church according to 4:23?

10. Based on what Paul writes in 2:24, what does he believe about his verdict?

MAKE IT COUNT

11. Who is your kindred spirit in the gospel? Take a moment right now to thank God for putting that person/those people in your life. If you don't yet have such a person, ask God to lead you to someone of the same mind and soul.

12. Are you committed to the advancement of the gospel whatever the cost? What is your next step of faith?

13. Who in your life is an example of Christlike humility? What about that person has impacted you the most?

DAY FOUR
TAKE IT IN
1. Read Philippians 2:12–30 AMP.

WRITE IT DOWN
2. Fill in the blanks for this week's memory verse: Philippians 2:12b–13 ESV.
Work _____ your own _____ with _____ and _____, for it is _____ who _____ in _____ both to _____ and to _____ for his _____ _____.

THINK IT THROUGH AND STORE IT UP
Focus on Philippians 2:25-30 ESV.

3. Who did Paul send and for what reason? (see Introduction question 9 and Phil. 2:26)

4. The only other mention of this person is in Philippians 4:18. Read this verse to understand what this person had previously done for the church and Paul. Write it here.

5. What five words does Paul use to describe this person?

6. Despite his own illness, who was this person concerned for and why?

7. What do Paul's words regarding Epaphroditus's healing indicate?

8. How are the people commanded to respond to Paul's messenger?

9. What do you learn from 2:30 about Epaphroditus's level of commitment to gospel work?

10. What specific qualities do the lives of these ordinary saints demonstrate?

Paul, Timothy, and Epaphroditus are all stellar examples of what it looks like to possess the mind of Christ as they do the work of Christ. They are equals in the body of Christ, constantly pouring themselves out for the kingdom of heaven. Each one is an ordinary person willing to be used by an extraordinary God.

MAKE IT COUNT

In addition to sharing the gospel, doing the work of Christ includes serving sacrificially. Doing the work of Christ includes going wherever God sends—whether across the room, across the street, or across the world. The work of

Christ includes showing up, meeting needs, and doing the will of God. The work of Christ is joining minds and hearts to be His hands and feet to the church and the world.

11. How are you investing and spending yourself for the sake of the gospel?

12. To emulate the ways of Paul, his gospel partners, and the Philippian church, in what ways do you commit to becoming more deeply connected to those you serve? In what ways do you commit to becoming more deeply connected to those with whom you serve?

13. How are you awakening to the work of Christ? In what ways does doing the work of Christ revive your soul?

14. Write out Philippians 2:12b–13 ESV from memory.

PRAYING WITH JOY

Lord Jesus,

I long to be obedient and to live a life that is faithful and consistent no matter who I'm with or where I am. Grant grace as I work out my salvation with fear and trembling, knowing the seriousness and importance of my faith. Work in me, Father, as only you can. Compel me to desire your will and to have a faith that works. Give me a willing, joyful spirit that resists grumbling and complaining or arguing. Purify my heart.

Thank you, God, for covering me in your righteousness and making me beautiful in your sight. Keep me rooted in my identity as your child. Cause me to radiate your love and to shine brightly in the darkness of this world. Keep me grounded in your Word. Thank you for those who invest in me. Humble me to be willing to pour myself out for your glory. Fill my heart with joy and gladness in your name.

I lay myself before You, God. Use this ordinary saint to do your will, I pray. Empower me to invest in others, raising up soul-sons and soul-daughters to know you and love you and share you. Grow my faith to be content where I am even when it's hard. Give me confidence in your plan always. Strengthen me to do what you want and go where you send—even if it is scary or risky—to bring glory to your name.

I am your beloved. Grow me in steadfastness, so that I am immovable, always abounding in the work of the Lord, knowing that in you my labor is not in vain (1 Cor. 15:58).

Thank you for your goodness to me, Jesus.

Amen.

NOTES

"Finish then Thy new creation,
Pure and spotless let us be;
Let us see Thy great salvation
Perfectly restored in Thee:
Changed from glory into glory,
Till in heav'n we take our place,
Till we cast our crowns before Thee,
Lost in wonder, love, and praise."

"Love Divine, All Loves Excelling"[14]

Week Six

**AWAKEN
TO
THE WORTH OF CHRIST**

Philippians 3:1–11

DAY ONE
TAKE IT IN
1. Read through the book of Philippians.
2. Read Philippians 3:1–11 ESV.

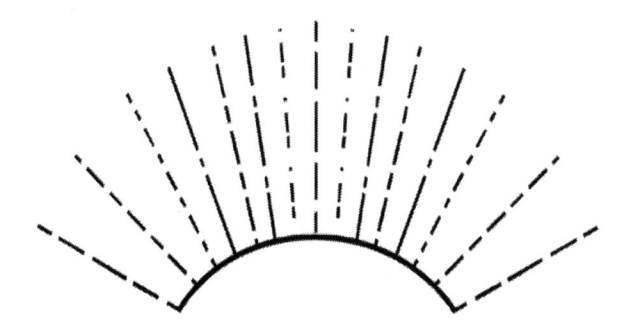

WRITE IT DOWN
3. Write down any initial thoughts, responses, and/or questions.

4. Highlight each of these recurring words in the ESV:
   Joy/Rejoice – YELLOW highlight
   Christ – YELLOW circle
   Flesh – RED circle
   Righteousness – BLUE underline

5. Write out this week's memory verse: Philippians 3:8 ESV. Write it down, study it, post it around your house. Make it a goal to memorize it this week.

DAY TWO
THINK IT THROUGH AND STORE IT UP

Focus on Philippians 3:1–3 ESV as you complete the following.

Paul begins this chapter with "Finally" even though he has much more to say before closing the letter. *Finally* is taken here to mean "well then," or "furthermore" as he transitions to a new section.

1. Paul didn't say "be happy in the Lord." What does he command? What is the difference between happiness and joy?

2. WORD STUDY: rejoice (3:1)
   Greek Word (Strong's #5463):

   Definition:

   Is this an active or passive verb? Why is that significant?

3. To whom is this kind of joy unique and why (consider the source)?

4. Write down what you learn about joy from the following verses:

   Psalm 4:7 -

   Psalm 16:11 -

   Habakkuk 3:18 -

   John 15:11 -

   Galatians 5:22–23 -

1 John 1:3–4 -

The treasure of Christ brings undeniable joy. Joy is not a simple gladness or happy feeling. Joy is a constant state of being, naturally flowing from our identity in Christ. This joy can be described as a supernatural excitement or an exhilaration of the soul. It is joy that is unspeakable and far surpasses anything this world has to offer. This treasure is simply divine.

"Then I will go to the altar of God, to God my exceeding joy, and I will praise you with the lyre, O God, my God" (Ps. 43:4).

5. What repeated command does Paul give in Philippians 3:2?

6. To whom is he referring (see 3:2 AMP)?

7. What three names does he give them? Why would he choose those descriptive words?

8. True circumcision is of the heart, and those who are justified by faith, Paul writes, "are the circumcision." What is the first phrase Paul uses in 3:3 to describe those who are the circumcision? What does Jesus say about this in John 4:24?

9. What is the second phrase Paul uses to describe true believers? The word *glory* here means "to boast" (see also 1 Cor. 1:31). What does this mean?

10. Write down the third phrase Paul uses to describe Christ-followers. What does this mean?

"The only good work that takes the sinner to heaven is the finished work of Christ on the cross."[15]

MAKE IT COUNT

Jesus is worthy of the excitement of our soul. He is most glorified when we are most excited and enthusiastic about Him;[16] when we find our satisfaction in Him; when we discover Him to be our greatest treasure.

11. Are you finding joy in the Lord? What does this look like for you in both good times and in hard times?

12. Are you vigilant in looking out for those who distort and pervert the truth? What is one practice that helps you stand firm?

13. "We are the circumcision, who worship by the Spirit of God and glory in Christ Jesus and put no confidence in the flesh" (Phil. 1:3). Is this true of you?

Describe your worship.

Practically speaking, how do you glory in Christ Jesus?

Where do you place your confidence? What is one practice that helps you stay grounded in Christ?

DAY THREE
TAKE IT IN
1. Read Philippians 3:1–11 AMP.

WRITE IT DOWN
2. This week's memory verse is Philippians 3:8 ESV. Fill in the blanks:
Indeed, I _____ everything as _____because of the surpassing _____ of knowing _____ _____ my Lord. For his _____ I have _____the loss of all _____ and count them as _____, in order that I may _____ Christ.

THINK IT THROUGH AND STORE IT UP
Focus on Philippians 3:4–8 ESV.

Paul has warned the church against those who believe human effort can secure salvation. If there was anyone who could be saved by outward conformity, it was Paul (rather, Saul). But he knows firsthand this cannot be done.

3. Paul gives several seemingly justifiable reasons for having confidence in the flesh.
Read 3:4-6 in the NLT and AMP for further understanding as you complete the following chart:

REASON (given in Phil.)	CROSS-REFERENCE	SIGNIFICANCE
	Gen. 17:12	
	Gen. 17:7	
	Deut. 33:12, 1 Kings 12:19-24	
	2 Cor. 11:22	
	Acts 26:5	
	Acts 26:11, Gal. 1:14	
	Matt. 5:20	

Paul once took great pride in being and achieving these things, viewing all these outward things as treasures and gain for himself. Then he saw the light…literally. (Read Acts 9 for details). And here Paul goes on to share his own story of being awakened by the treasure of Christ. The word "But" he uses to begin Philippians 3:7 indicates opposition between the past and the present. As Paul continues, we begin to see a radically transformed life.

4. WORD STUDY: gain (3:7)
   Greek Word (Strong's #2771):

   Definition:

   Where else has Paul used this word in his letter to the Philippians? (Hint: see memory verses for Week 3.)

   Look up Mark 8:36 to see this word used as a verb meaning "to acquire" or "win." How are these verses connected?

5. What does "for the sake of Christ" mean to you?

6. What does Paul consider loss compared to Christ? Ponder this.

7. Read Philippians 3:8 aloud in each of these translations: ESV, NLT, and AMP. Now write the key phrase here. This is the crux of this study. Spend time right now praying over these words.

8. WORD STUDY: rubbish (3:8)
   Greek Word (Strong's # 4657):

   Definition:

9. For what reason does Paul consider all the former things as rubbish?

10. Explain what it means to gain Christ.

    MAKE IT COUNT
    Counting all other things as loss—worthless and detestable—for the sake of Christ is an ongoing process. We must practically choose to hold Christ as our greatest treasure every day.

11. In what things other than Christ are you tempted to put your confidence?

12. Are you simply setting other things aside, or truly counting everything as loss compared to knowing Christ? What is one action step you can take this week to refocus your eyes on the beauty and richness of Jesus?

13. Do you tend to get complacent or drowsy in your relationship with Christ? How can you awaken to the surpassing worth of Christ?

"…that their hearts may be encouraged, being knit together in love, to reach all the riches of full assurance of understanding and the knowledge of God's mystery, which is Christ, in whom are hidden all the treasures of wisdom and knowledge." – Col. 2:2–3

DAY FOUR
TAKE IT IN
1. Read Philippians 3:1–11 NLT.

   WRITE IT DOWN
2. Fill in the blanks for this week's memory verse: Philippians 3:8 ESV.
   _____, I _____ everything as _____ because of the _____ worth of _____ Christ Jesus my _____. For _____ sake I have _____ the _____ of all _____ and _____ them as _____, in _____ that I may gain _____.

   THINK IT THROUGH AND STORE IT UP
   Focus on Philippians 3:9–11 ESV.

3. What is Paul's end goal as stated in 3:9? What does this imply (see 3:9 NLT)?

4. WORD STUDY: righteousness (3:9)
   Greek Word (Strong's #1343):

   Definition:

5. Define faith. (See also Heb. 11:1.)

6. What is the difference between righteousness from the law and righteousness in Christ? (See also Rom. 3:21–28.)

7. Paul earnestly desires to know Christ. Read Philippians 3:10 AMP. How does this help you better understand what it means to know Christ?

   Knowing Jesus is "the unique experience of God that is totally other, entirely foreign to us and yet captivating to us, taking us away, transforming us, moving us, stirring us, and spiritually and sweetly discombobulating us."[17] Are you ready to truly know Jesus?

8. Knowing Christ also includes knowing the power of His resurrection. Read the following verses and note what you learn about this resurrection power for both our present and our future:

   Romans 8:11 -

Ephesians 2:4–6 -

Colossians 3:1–3 -

9. Paul longs to experience Christ intimately, even sharing in His sufferings. What does Scripture tell us about suffering for the sake of Christ?

    Matthew 5:10 -

    2 Corinthians 4:17 -

    Colossians 1:24 -

10. Is Paul uncertain about his own resurrection from the dead (see also 2 Cor. 4:13–14)? Why might he choose this wording as he writes Philippians 3:11?

MAKE IT COUNT

11. How were you first awakened to the truth of the gospel? How is your life changing as a result? If you are still asleep to this treasure, ask God to open your eyes. Pray that Paul's words in Philippians 3:8 will be the cry of your heart. Talk with believing friends who will point you to Jesus. God has extended the invitation; the treasure is yours for the taking.

12. What revives and stirs your soul for the affections of Christ?

13. If Christ is your greatest treasure, He is also the lover of your soul. "I am my beloved's and my beloved is mine" (Song of Sol. 6:3). Write a love letter to the One who gave Himself to give you everything.

14. Write out Philippians 3:8 ESV from memory.

PRAYING WITH JOY

Lord God,

    This is the day that you have made. I will rejoice and be glad in it! Oh Jesus, give me eyes to see and a mind to discern truth from all that is false. Protect me as I remain vigilant, aware of those who are out to deceive. Cut away from my heart and mind all the things that distract me from you, God. I worship you, Lord, in spirit and truth. I worship you, Jesus, who is the truth. My glory is in Christ alone, not in any fleshly act or circumstance. I too have reasons I could boast. But none of those things matter—they are all loss compared to Christ. You are my everything. Knowing you, Lord, far surpasses anything I could possess or use as a replacement for you. Knowing you—being known by you—is my beautiful treasure.

    Thank you, Jesus, for clothing me in your righteousness, for I could never achieve it on my own. I am beyond grateful for the confidence I have in you. Draw me to yourself, that I may be found in you, my Lord and Savior. Grow my faith to know you more intimately, to experience the power of your resurrection. And God, I know that also means suffering with you and dying with you so that I might also rise with you. Preserve me, Lord. Give me faith to stand firm. Help me to count everything as loss because of the surpassing worth of knowing Jesus Christ my Lord.

    You are exalted, for you dwell on high; You will fill me with justice and righteousness, and you will be the stability of my times, abundance of salvation, wisdom, and knowledge; the fear of the Lord is my treasure (Is. 33:5-6).

I love you, Lord Jesus.

Amen.

NOTES

"My Jesus I love Thee,
I know Thou art mine;
For Thee all the follies of sin I resign;
My gracious Redeemer,
My Savior art Thou;
If ever I loved Thee, my Jesus 'tis now."

"My Jesus I Love Thee"[18]

Week Seven

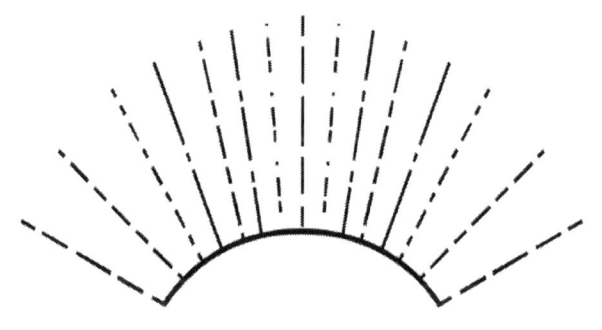

**AWAKEN
TO
THE PRIZE OF CHRIST**

Philippians 3:12–4:1

DAY ONE
TAKE IT IN
1. Read through the book of Philippians.
2. Read Philippians 3:12 - 4:1 ESV.

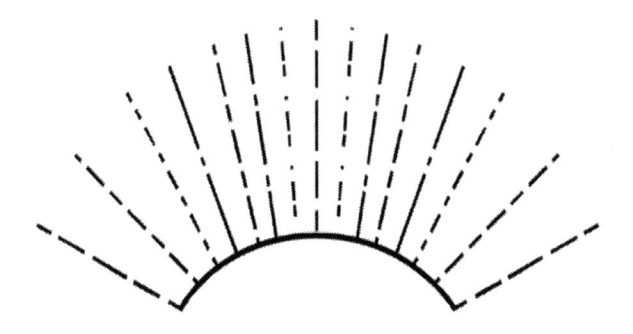

WRITE IT DOWN
3. Write down any initial thoughts, responses, and/or questions.

4. Highlight each of these recurring words in the ESV:
   Christ – YELLOW circle

5. Write a summary sentence for 3:12-16 and for verses 3:17 - 4:1.

6. Write out this week's memory verse: Philippians 3:13b–14 ESV. Write it down, study it, post it around your house. Make it a goal to memorize it this week.

DAY TWO
THINK IT THROUGH AND STORE IT UP

Focus on Philippians 3:12–16 ESV as you complete the following.

Apparently, there are some within the Philippian church who believe they have reached perfection in the Christian life. As Paul addresses the whole body of believers, he has these readers in mind.

1. Does Paul believe he has reached spiritual perfection? How do you know?

2. WORD STUDY- press on (3:12)
   Greek Word (Strong's #1377):

   Definition:

3. What motivates Paul to press on?

4. "One thing" is a phrase also used in other passages of Scripture. Who spoke about this in Mark 10:21 and Luke 10:41-42? What can you infer is the one thing?

   Look up and write out Psalm 27:4.

   What is the common thread of these verses including Philippians 3:13?

While we are called to be in fellowship and community, ministering to those needing to experience the power of the gospel, we must also be careful not to get involved in or distracted by so many other things that we miss our one thing, Jesus Christ!

5. What actions does Paul continually do according to 3:13, and why is each significant?

6. What is Paul's end goal?

7. Based on your understanding, what is the "upward call of God"?

Pressing on is a continual action that signifies constant pursuit of Jesus, intentionally laying aside every weight, every lesser thing, and all the sin that so easily entangles. It is daily moving forward, eyes and heart laser-focused on the one thing: the prize of Christ.

8. Some Bible translations use the word *perfect* again in 3:15. What word is used in the ESV? How do the spiritually mature think differently than the spiritually immature?

9. What does Paul believe about believers who may disagree? (See also 3:15 NLT.)

10. To what should the Philippian church hold true? What does this mean? (See also 3:16 NLT.)

MAKE IT COUNT

Truly knowing God always leaves us aching for more of God. Understanding His constant pursuit of us compels us to press on in pursuit of Him. We live with holy discontent, continually seeking to be caught up in the mind and ways of Christ.

11. Do you continue to be awed by the power of the gospel? Does the truth of the Good News still get to you in a way that leaves you with a holy discontent? How do you respond?

12. Paul urges his readers to "forget what is behind." Truth be told, this includes both positive and negative experiences. But it does not mean we fail to remember. It means we choose not to hold onto the things that have already happened as predictors or guarantees of the things that lie ahead. The mistakes of our past do not disqualify us for the future. In the same way, past victories or accomplishments do not secure our tomorrows. We live in the grace God gives today, eagerly following after the things of heaven in the present. What are some highs and lows from your past that might distract or diminish your current pursuit of Jesus?

13. How can you press on like Jesus Christ is the only prize? What does that look like in real life?

DAY THREE
TAKE IT IN
1. Read Philippians 3:12–4:1 AMP.

WRITE IT DOWN
2. This week's memory verse is Philippians 3:13b–14 ESV. Fill in the blanks:
But one _____ I do: _____ what lies _____ and straining _____ to what lies _____, I _____ on toward the _____ for the prize of the upward _____ of God in Christ _____.

THINK IT THROUGH AND STORE IT UP
Focus on Philippians 3:17–19 ESV.

3. What does Paul invite the believers to do and why?

4. Based on what you know about Paul and his gospel partners, what kind of example has the church been given?

5. What grieves Paul in this passage?

6. What does it mean to be "enemies of the cross of Christ"? (See also 3:18 AMP and NLT.)

7. What will be the end for the enemies of Christ?

   What is the end for those He calls His own? (See Heb. 11:16; Col. 1:5.)

8. Who/what do enemies of Christ worship?

   How does this compare to Christ's beloved ones? (See Prov. 13:25; Gal. 5:16.)

9. In what do the enemies of Christ find glory?

   What is the boast of believers? (See Ps. 34:2; Gal. 6:14.)

10. What is the focus of the minds of those who are enemies of Christ?

    On what do the faithful focus their minds? (See Rom. 8:5; Col. 3:2.)

MAKE IT COUNT

11. In 1 Corinthians 11:1 Paul writes, "And you should imitate me, just as I imitate Christ." In today's passage Paul again urges his readers to follow his godly example. Whose example are you following? Who do you look to as a spiritual champion and why? In what ways does this person point you to Jesus, our only perfect example?

12. Who do you know living as an enemy of the cross of Christ? Does your heart grieve for this person and the way their decision might also be impacting others? Reach out to him/her this week with a gospel truth or godly word of encouragement. Pray earnestly for him/her.

13. Do an honest assessment of your own life. Who are you worshiping in everyday life? Who/what has become a god in your life? Where is the focus of your mind? If spiritual apathy is leading you away from Christ, confess it to the Lord. Ask God to revive your heart and awaken your mind to the things of heaven.

DAY FOUR
TAKE IT IN
1. Read Philippians 3:12–4:1 NLT.

WRITE IT DOWN
2. Fill in the blanks for this week's memory verse: Philippians 3:13b–14 ESV.
   But _____ thing I do: _____ what _____ behind and _____ forward to what lies _____, I _____ on toward the _____ for the _____ of the _____ call of _____ in _____ _____.

THINK IT THROUGH AND STORE IT UP
Focus on Philippians 3:20–4:1 ESV.

3. What is our identity and home as believers?

4. What does the Bible tell us in the following verses about who we are and where we're headed?

   Hebrews 11:13 –

   1 Peter 2:11 –

   Colossians 1:3-5 –

   Hebrews 11:10 –

5. Who are we awaiting and what is the significance of all the titles Paul uses in Philippians 3:20 to describe this person?

6. What will Christ do for those who believe when He returns? (See also 1 Cor. 15:52–53.)

7. What does His power enable Him to do? (See also 1 Cor. 15:27–28; Heb. 2:8.) What does this mean?

8. How does Paul address his readers in Philippians 4:1? What does this continue to indicate?

9. What two nouns does Paul use to describe the Philippian church? Based on Paul's connection to this church, why would he choose these words?

10. What does Paul command the church to do and why (review 3:20-21 and the connecting word "therefore")?

MAKE IT COUNT

11. What does it mean to you to be a citizen of heaven? How does this impact your life on earth?

12. Who have you discipled or are you discipling? How does their faith bring joy to your life?

13. Jesus died to save you from your sin. He rose again, eternally conquering sin and death. He promises to continue His work in you until you stand before Him face to face. In the blink of an eye, He will transform even your body to be like His by the very word of His power. And you will spend eternity enjoying unhindered communion with the King of kings and Lord of lords. How does your knowledge of these glorious truths alter your anticipation of the future? What does it mean to you to awaken to the prize of Christ?

14. Write out Philippians 3:13b–14 ESV from memory.

PRAYING WITH JOY

Oh Lord,

I am well aware that I am a work in progress. I am nowhere near perfect, and I never will be until I step into glory. But I press on—moving forward to receive one day all that is mine because I belong to you. Help me, Jesus, to forget what is behind me and strain for and run toward what is yet to come. Forgive me, Father, when I lose my zeal and give in to complacency. Give me strength and courage to press on with purpose and passion to reach the goal—the prize of Christ Himself. Grow me in spiritual maturity to influence others to have this same attitude. Continue to reveal yourself and your ways as I seek to follow you, Lord. Let me hold tightly to what I know and to grow to know you more each day.

Lord, give me a heart and mind like Paul, who kept his eyes on you always. May I too be an example of what it looks like to be a faithful follower, walking in obedience, sharing my faith even when I find myself in a difficult season. Set me apart, Father, from those who walk as enemies of the cross. Instead of destruction, grant me complete sanctification in you. May you always be my one and only God.

Forgive me for giving in to lesser things. My glory is in you alone, Lord, for you have covered my shame. Set my mind on things above, my eyes fixed only on you, Jesus. I wait for you, God my Savior, as I long for my heavenly home. The world is not where I belong, but I know you have me here for such a time as this.

Oh Father, you are making me like Jesus, and one day even this body of mine, flawed and frail, will be transformed to be like the glorious body of Christ by your matchless power. Give me such deep love for the saints that I plead with them for the sake of eternity to stand firm, even as I, your beloved, also strive to do. I love you, Jesus, and want my life to emulate the great heroes of faith—that others might know you better because they have known me.

Whom have I in heaven but you, Jesus? And there is nothing on earth that I desire besides you. My flesh and my heart may fail, but God, you are the strength of my heart. You are my portion and my prize for all eternity (Ps. 73:25-26).

In Jesus' name I pray,

Amen.

NOTES

"I'm pressing on the upward way,
New heights I'm gaining every day;
Still praying as I'm onward bound,
"Lord, plant my feet on higher ground."

"Higher Ground"[19]

Week Eight

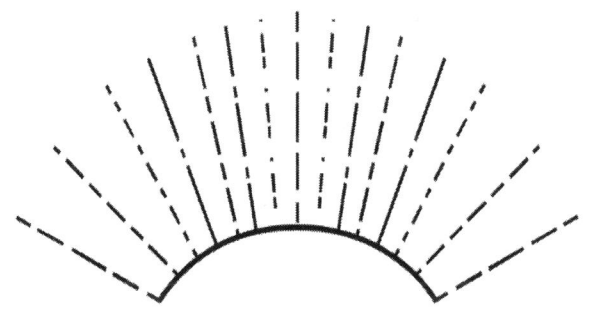

**AWAKEN
TO
THE JOY OF CHRIST**

Philippians 4:2–9

DAY ONE
TAKE IT IN
1. Read through the book of Philippians.
2. Read Philippians 4:2–9 ESV.

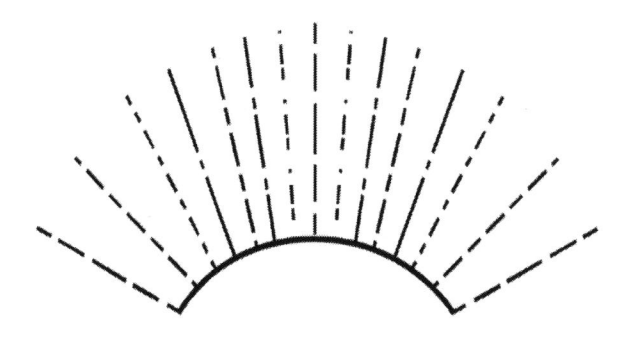

   WRITE IT DOWN
3. Write down any initial thoughts, responses, and/or questions.

4. Highlight each of these recurring words in the ESV:
   Gospel – ORANGE highlight
   Joy/Rejoice – YELLOW highlight
   Pray/Prayer – PURPLE circle
   Christ – YELLOW circle

5. Write out this week's memory verse: Philippians 4:8 ESV. Write it down, study it, post it around your house. Make it a goal to memorize it this week.

DAY TWO
THINK IT THROUGH AND STORE IT UP

Focus on Philippians 4:2–3 ESV as you complete the following.

Paul has commanded the church to stand firm in the Lord, to hold their position by divine strength. In this week's passage, he explains several ways to honor this instruction.

1. WORD STUDY – entreat (4:2)
   Greek Word (Strong's #3870):

   Definition:

   The fact that Paul uses this word to address each woman individually shows the importance and potential impact of the matter at hand and the responsibility of each to seek reconciliation.

2. Paul calls out each of these women by name. What does this tell you about their roles in the Philippian church?

3. How might an issue between two individuals impact the body of believers?

4. What does Paul mean when he tells these women to "agree in the Lord"? (See also 4:2 NLT and AMP.)

5. There is scholarly debate over who Paul addresses as "true companion" in 4:3. Commentators say it could have been Luke, Epaphroditus, Syzgos (whose name actually means "companion"), or the church as a whole. But more important than the identity is the task/role Paul seeks of this true companion. What does he ask this third party to do?

6. Paul described Euodia and Syntyche as having "labored side by side with me." The original language says they "shared in my struggle in the cause of the gospel." Explain what this means. (See also Phil.1:3–5, 27.)

7. Scripture tells us nothing else about Clement. Given Paul's mention of him in 4:3, who might he be?

8. What does Paul say about everyone he mentions in these verses?

9. What do you know about the book of life? (See also Dan. 12:1; Lk. 10:20; Rev. 21:23–27.)

10. Read Philippians 4:2–3 again. What can you determine is the first way Paul urges this church to stand firm?

MAKE IT COUNT

11. The dispute between Euodia and Syntyche was not one of theological discrepancy. It was a clash of personality or preference. Unfortunately their disagreement grew big enough to affect the larger church, significant enough that

Paul (800 miles away) had heard about it. Are you at odds with a brother or sister in Christ? What steps can you take this week to reconcile before it impacts a larger body of believers?

12. How are you helping to maintain and/or restore unity within the church? Be specific.

13. From the beginning of time, God has called His people to be in community. We were never meant to run or work alone. God called Euodia and Syntyche to partner with Paul in kingdom work. God continues to call men and women to labor side by side in the work of the gospel. How can you be part of kingdom work within your church? In your community? Across the world?

"A divided church is a terrible witness. Where people see in a church anger, dissention, inability to reconcile, and the holding of grudges, they do not see Christ as beautiful.... Grace put into practice toward unity in fellowship with each other produces joy. When the people in a church dwell together in the unity of the gospel and together pursue the building up of one another in love, they are providing fertile soil for the roots of deep joy."[20] May we live and minister in unity so that our joy is unhindered and our Jesus is seen as the beautiful One He is.

DAY THREE
TAKE IT IN
1. Read Philippians 4:2–9 AMP.

WRITE IT DOWN
2. This week's memory verse is Philippians 4:8 ESV. Fill in the blanks:
Finally, _____, whatever is _____, whatever is _____, whatever is _____, whatever is _____, whatever is _____, whatever is _____, if there is any _____ if there is anything worthy of _____, think about _____ things.

THINK IT THROUGH AND STORE IT UP
Focus on Philippians 4:4-7 ESV.

3. What is Paul's repeated command in 4:4? Is Paul telling us to be happy in and about all things? Explain.

4. The joy of the Lord has been impacting the lives of God's people since the beginning of time. Look up the following verses and note specific ways this joy is and should continue to be expressed:

Jeremiah 31:9–13 NLT –

Zephaniah 3:14–17 –

Luke 1:44 –

Philippians 1:4 –

The joy of the Lord impacts how we do all of life. Joy is both an inner delight and an outward exuberance making the Christian life attractive and appealing to those around us. In addition to that, we have a God who rejoices over us (with loud singing!) as we delight in Him. What an awesome God!

5. WORD STUDY: reasonableness (4:5)
   Greek Word (Strong's #1933):

   Definition:

6. Explain how experiencing joy leads to reasonableness/a gentle spirit.

7. "The Lord is at hand" can mean both the presence of the Lord is near and the coming of Christ will be soon. How are both of these interpretations cause for rejoicing?

8. WORD STUDY: anxious (4:6)
   Greek Word (Strong's #3309):

   Definition:

   Where else have we seen this same word (hint: review week 5)? How is it the same or different?

9. How should we handle our anxieties and worry? What elements should this include, according to 4:6? Explain the importance of each.

"Prayer is a conversation with...the supreme person of the universe, who can hear, know, understand, care about, and respond to the concerns that otherwise would sink people into despair."[21] God invites (and Paul commands) believers to have a conversation with Him about all the concerns and cares and celebrations of our minds and hearts.

10. What does Paul say believers will receive as a result? Describe the beauty and power of this gift.

Paul has urged the church at Philippi to stand firm in the Lord by choosing reconciliation instead of resentment when disagreements arise; by finding joy in Christ despite difficult circumstances; by determining to pray (not panic!), worship (not worry!), and exude faith (not fear!) when anxieties threaten to overwhelm us. We too can lean into His nearness, pour out our hearts, remember His goodness, and experience His peace.

MAKE IT COUNT

11. Share a time you allowed your circumstances to steal your joy. Also share a time when your joy remained firmly rooted in Christ despite your circumstances. What have you learned from each of those situations?

12. My counseling pastor friend often advises, "Respond thoughtfully, don't react emotionally."[22] Describe both an emotional reaction you have experienced and a thoughtful response you have offered in specific situations. Was God honored? What impact did your thoughts, words, and subsequent actions have in each of those situations?

13. The overwhelming peace of God stands guard over your heart (emotions) and your mind (thoughts). How have you experienced this divine protection in your life?

DAY FOUR
TAKE IT IN
1. Read Philippians 4:2–9 NLT.

WRITE IT DOWN
2. Fill in the blanks for this week's memory verse: Philippians 4:8 ESV.

_____, brothers, _____ is true, whatever is _____, _____is just, whatever is _____ _____ is lovely, whatever is _____, if _____ is any _____, if there is _____ worthy of _____, _____ about these _____.

THINK IT THROUGH AND STORE IT UP
Focus on Philippians 4:8–9 ESV.

Paul's final exhortations to the Philippian church on standing firm in the Lord begin with right thinking. *To think* means "to dwell on" or "to put your focus on."

3. Why would Paul address right thinking before right living?

4. Paul says to "think on these things." What are the first three of these things? Give an example of each.

   Whatever is _____
   This is real and genuine; it is not false:

   Whatever is _____
   This is respectable and dignified:

   Whatever is _____
   This is holy and upright:

5. What are the next three things in the list, and what else does Scripture say about these things?

   Whatever is _____
   2 Corinthians 7:11 -

   Matthew 5:8 -

   Whatever is _____
   Psalm 84:1 –

   Psalm 96:6 –

   Whatever is _____
   Psalm 145:3-4 –

Proverbs 31:25–27 –

6. Using the same language he used in the beginning of chapter 2 ("if there is") Paul is not questioning but rather stating two more things on which to focus our minds. Using a dictionary or in your own words, define the last two words from Paul's list.

   Excellent:

   Praiseworthy:

   All these things point us back to Christ, whose mind we are to emulate. Write Philippians 2:5 in your own words.

7. What does the Bible say about the minds of God's people in the following verses?
   Matthew 22:37 –

   Romans 8:5—6 –

   Ephesians 4:22–24 –

   1 Peter 1:13 –

8. What command does Paul give in verse 9?

9. Describe what Paul commands the church to live out.

   What have they learned from Paul?

What have they received from Paul?

What have they heard from Paul?

What have they seen in Paul?

10. What is the promised result of a life of right thinking and right living?

Numerous studies reveal that a significant percentage of our thoughts are negative. We are often not even aware of this tragic reality. We will become in practice what fills our minds in thought. Therefore, we must be intentional to "take every thought captive and make it obedient to Christ" (2 Cor. 10:5). The thoughts we entertain become ideas we believe. What we believe then directly impacts the words we say and the actions we take. If we desire to live a godly life, we must fill our minds with godly thoughts.

"You keep him in perfect peace whose mind is stayed on you, because he trusts in you" (Is. 26:3).

MAKE IT COUNT

11. What are some specific ways you can think on the things of Philippians 4:8 as you go about your daily life?

12. Give a personal example of how wrong thinking has led you to wrong living and how right thinking leads to right living.

13. In His presence there is fullness of joy. The joy of Christ is a beautiful and wonderful gift produced in us by the Holy Spirit. Are you awake to His joy? Find a favorite photo, image, or Bible verse that brings you much joy. Use it as the background on your computer or phone. Whenever you see it, ask God to revive the passion of your soul as you take delight in Him.

14. Write out Philippians 4:8 ESV from memory.

PRAYING WITH JOY

Father God,

Please forgive me when I allow silly arguments to disrupt the unity of your church. Humble my heart to seek reconciliation with my brothers and sisters in Christ. Help me to remember that we are gospel partners holding the treasure of Christ in common. Help me to choose joy—if for no other reason than because I am in you, Lord!

Grant me a gentle and reasonable spirit that is noticeable to those around me. You are near; therefore, remove my anxieties and fill me with yourself. I pour myself out before you—all my requests and concerns and praises—every single one, with thanksgiving, for you are a good and faithful God. Thank you for your gift of peace that guards my heart and my mind. Overwhelm me with that peace in the chaos of my day.

Oh Lord, I want to focus my mind and heart on the things of you, but I am so prone to wander. Saturate my mind on these things, Lord Jesus: whatever is true—not lies or what-ifs, whatever is honorable—only what glorifies you, nothing shameful or sinful, whatever is just—not vengeful or angry but right and good, knowing you are the God of justice.

Remove any impure thoughts, so my thoughts include only what is clean and pure and holy. Renew my mind with that which is lovely—not ugly thoughts full of anger or jealousy or destruction, but what is beautiful, kind, and gentle. Restore my mind with things commendable—thoughts of integrity and solid character; excellent—wonderful, good, magnificent things; and guard me against entertaining thoughts that do not deserve praise.

Give me strength and patience Lord, to live out what I've learned and know what will bring you glory. I want to follow Paul's example in living out my faith in every aspect of life. Overwhelm me with your peace as I follow you.

You have awakened my heart and revived my soul; therefore, "I will shout for joy and sing your praises, for you have ransomed me" (Ps. 71:23 NLT).

Thank you, Lord.

Amen.

NOTES

"Joyful, joyful, we adore Thee,
God of glory, Lord of love;
Hearts unfold like flowers before Thee,
Opening to the sun above.
Melt the clouds of sin and sadness;
Drive the dark of doubt away;
Give of immortal gladness,
Fill us with the light of day!"

"Joyful, Joyful, We Adore Thee"[23]

Week Nine

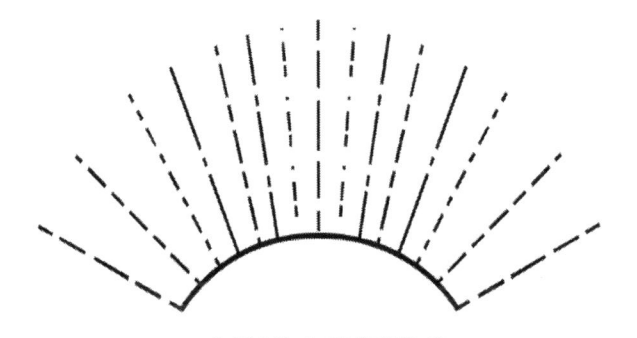

**AWAKEN
TO
THE PROVISION OF CHRIST**

Philippians 4:10–23

DAY ONE
TAKE IT IN
1. Read through the book of Philippians.
2. Read Philippians 4:10–23 ESV.

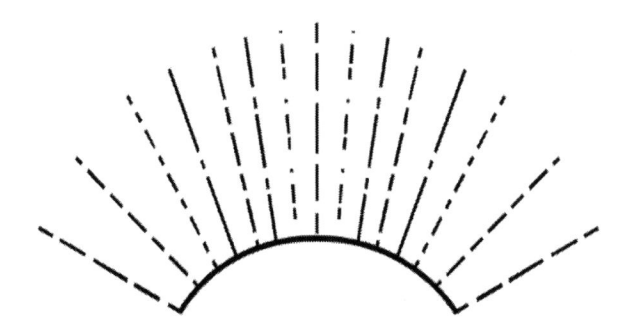

WRITE IT DOWN
3. Write down any initial thoughts, responses, and/or questions.

4. Highlight each of these recurring words in the ESV:
   Joy/Rejoice – YELLOW highlight
   Gospel – ORANGE highlight
   Christ – YELLOW circle

5. Write out this week's memory verse: Philippians 4:19–20 ESV. Write it down, study it, post it around your house. Make it a goal to memorize it this week.

DAY TWO
THINK IT THROUGH AND STORE IT UP

Focus on Philippians 4:10–13 ESV as you complete the following.

Paul has given the church several practical ways to stand firm in the faith. As he finishes this letter, he shifts his focus from the "how" to the "why." Paul is confident this church can stand firm because God is faithful. Paul has experienced firsthand God's providence over him, God's provision for him, and God's power in him.

1. What was Paul's response to the concern of the Philippian church?

2. WORD STUDY: revive (4:10)
   Greek Word (Strong's #330):

   Definition:

3. What outward display demonstrated the Philippians' concern? (See Phil 4:18).

4. What does it mean that the Philippians "had no opportunity"?

5. What vital heart posture has Paul found in all situations?

6. How did he come to this heart posture according to 4:11? What additional truth does Paul share about this in 1 Timothy 6:6?

7. In what circumstances does Paul exude this heart posture? (See Phil. 4:12.)

8. Paul's life has consisted of steepest mountains and deepest valleys. He mentions a few general highs and lows from his life and ministry. List those from 4:12 and describe what each means:

HIGHS	LOWS

9. Philippians 4:13 is one of the most misunderstood and misappropriated verses in the Bible. How does the context help to accurately interpret this verse?

10. Where does Paul get the strength to find contentment no matter his circumstances?

The word used for *content* indicates a level of self-sufficiency. Yet because of Paul's position in Christ and knowledge of God as the all-sufficient One, the great apostle experienced a contentment the world could never know. Essentially what Paul says in these verses is this: *I was never really in need of anything. I've seen God take little and make it enough, even more than enough sometimes. I can live with almost nothing because it is all rubbish compared to having and knowing Christ. I am also satisfied when my cup runs over and I have plenty. Through the ups and downs of life, I have learned the secret of contentment in every situation. I can endure—and even thrive—in all situations because it is Christ who infuses me with strength.*

MAKE IT COUNT

11. Whose godly concern for you and for the gospel causes you to rejoice greatly in the Lord? How is their concern and your joy expressed?

12. Have you found the secret of contentment? When do you struggle to remain content? What life circumstances has God used to teach and grow you in this?

13. Explain what Philippians 4:13 means and does not mean in light of what you've learned from this lesson.

DAY THREE
TAKE IT IN
1. Read Philippians 4:10–23 NLT.

WRITE IT DOWN
2. This week's memory verse is Philippians 4:19–20 ESV. Fill in the blanks:
   And my _____ will _____ every _____ of yours according to his _____ in glory in _____ Jesus. To our _____ and Father be _____ forever and _____. Amen.

THINK IT THROUGH AND STORE IT UP
Focus on Philippians 4:14–19 ESV.

3. What does 4:14–16 reveal about Paul's history with the Philippian church?

4. What does Paul seek instead of the gift itself?

5. Remembering that he is in chains, how does Paul describe his situation in 4:18?

6. What does Paul say about the gifts he received from the church at Philippi? Look up the following verses where Paul uses this same type of language: Romans 12:1; 2 Corinthians 2:14; Ephesians 5:2. What does this imply?

7. Paul makes a powerful statement about God in Philippians 4:19. Write it below. How can Paul so confidently make such a statement?

8. Jehovah-Jireh is the Hebrew name used in Genesis 22:13–14 when God gives early evidence of this specific character attribute. What does Jehovah-Jireh mean according to these verses? Literally translated, this means "the Lord will see to it."

9. God's provision doesn't always look like what we expect. We must keep in mind that we can trust God to meet our needs, which is not the same as giving us

everything we want or acting in ways we think He should. God's riches are quite different than those of the world.

What do you learn about the riches of God from these verses: Romans 10:12, Ephesians 2:7, 3:16, and Colossians 2:2–3?

10. Read Deuteronomy 8:1-18 NLT. In this passage, what does Moses call God's people to remember? Reread Philippians 4:10–19. Paul is likely remembering his own experiences as he writes to the Philippians. What common themes and threads do you detect? What message do both Moses and Paul long to convey to God's people?

MAKE IT COUNT

11. Give specific situations when God was faithful to provide for you. How did He "see to it" on your behalf?

12. What is one way you can give ministry support and to whom? Ask God to make it a fragrant offering, a sacrifice acceptable and pleasing in His sight.

13. How is Paul's example of trust and contentment in a faithful God awakening you to the provision of Christ? How does this revive your soul?

DAY FOUR
TAKE IT IN
1. Read Philippians 4:10–23 AMP.

WRITE IT DOWN
2. Fill in the blanks for this week's memory verse: Philippians 4:19–20 ESV.
   _____ my God _____ supply _____ need of _____ according to his _____ in_____ in Christ _____. To our _____ and _____be _____ _____ and ever. _____.

THINK IT THROUGH AND STORE IT UP
Focus on Philippians 4:20–23 ESV.

3. What is the end goal of all personal and ministry efforts as Paul reiterates in 4:20?

4. How does Paul refer to believers in 4:21?

5. WORD STUDY: saints (4:21)
   Greek Word (Strong's #40):

   Definition:

It is astonishing that even though we are sinners, in Christ we are identified as holy ones! In our flawed lives, God commands us to "be holy, for I am holy" (Lev. 11:44), and Paul reassures us that "He chose us in him before the foundation of the world, that we should be holy and blameless before him" (Eph. 1:4). To be a saint does not mean we are perfect, but it does mean we are daily being transformed into the likeness of our perfect Lord.

6. Paul is careful to clarify in Philippians 4:21 which saints he wishes to be greeted. What word does he use and why would this be his desire?

7. Who are "all the saints" who send greetings?

8. Even while under house arrest, Paul is reaching people with the gospel. Who does he specifically mention in 4:22? Why is this significant?

9. As is common for Paul, he bookends this letter. He begins and ends with grace. This isn't simply a routine style of writing or a godly choice of words. This is intentional. What is the desire of Paul's heart as he opens, writes, and closes this letter to the Philippians?

10. Review Paul's opening greeting in 1:2. Now reread his closing greeting in 4:20, 23. Who/what is the focus of this letter from beginning to end?

MAKE IT COUNT

11. Do you view yourself and other believers as saints? Explain your answer.

12. How are you allowing even the difficult circumstances of your life to awaken your desire to share the gospel with others? Who is "Caesar's household" in your life (those you are unlikely to minister to if not for a specific and possibly unwanted circumstance)?

13. How are you continually growing and living in the grace of Christ?

14. Write out Philippians 4:19–20 ESV from memory.

"Will you not revive us again, that your people may rejoice in you? Show us your steadfast love, O LORD, and grant us your salvation." – Ps. 85:6–7

PRAYING WITH JOY

All-sufficient God,

Mold my heart to be tender toward the needs of others, using every opportunity to encourage, support, and do good. I have also experienced times of need and times of abundance. You have taught me to be content in either situation because you have always provided for me. No matter my circumstance you never change, and because you have been faithful in every circumstance, I know that I will be okay. I can endure, survive, and even thrive in all things because you are my strength. Thank you for this truth. Forgive me when I twist this verse to say something it never said or never meant.

Lord, give me practical faith that willingly and generously comes alongside others proclaiming and living gospel truth. May I eagerly partner with others, offering support to see your work accomplished so that the world may know you. Bring forth fruit from my life that evidences my faith. Cleanse me, Lord, so that what I offer you will be pleasing and acceptable in your sight. Thank you for supplying my needs with your steadfast provision. Grow my faith to trust you daily, believing that you will do all that you have said.

Thank you for your abundant blessings to me, so that in all things and at all times, I have everything I need, and am able to abound in every good work (2 Cor. 9:8).

In me and in all this, Lord, be glorified.

Amen.

AWAKEN

NOTES

"Great is Thy faithfulness!
Great is Thy faithfulness!
Morning by morning new mercies I see;
All I have needed
Thy hand hath provided.
Great is Thy Faithfulness,
Lord, unto me!"

"Great is Thy Faithfulness"[25]

Week Ten

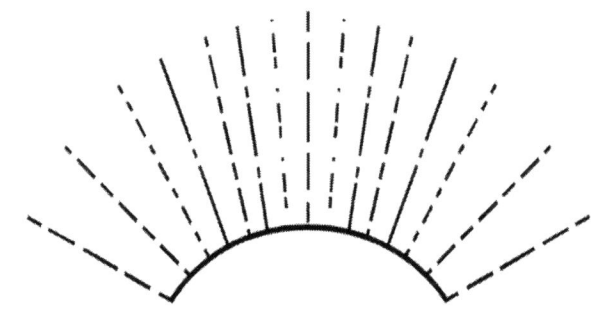

THE ABSOLUTE TREASURE OF CHRIST

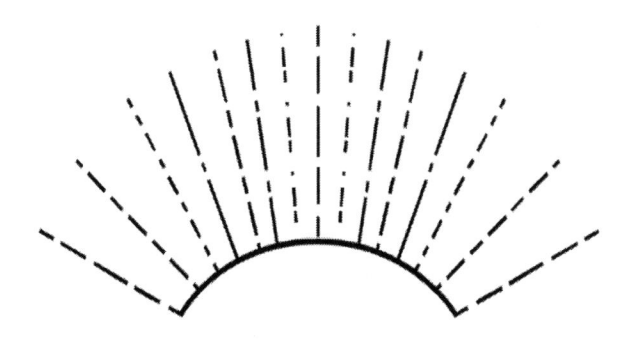

TAKE IT IN
1. Read through the book of Philippians one more time (your preferred translation).

WRITE IT DOWN
2. Summarize each section and give at least one takeaway after multiple readings and weeks of study.

Awaken to the Fellowship of Christ: Philippians 1:3–11

Awaken to the Satisfaction of Christ: Philippians 1:12–30

Awaken to the Mind of Christ: Philippians 2:1–11

Awaken to the Work of Christ: Philippians 2:12–30

Awaken to the Worth of Christ: Philippians 3:1–11

Awaken to the Prize of Christ: Philippians 3:12–4:1

Awaken to the Joy of Christ: Philippians 4:2–9

Awaken to the Provision of Christ: Philippians 4:10–23

3. Have you memorized the weekly verses? Write them below.

   Philippians 1:6

   Philippians 1:20–21

   Philippians 2:1–2

   Philippians 2:12b–13

   Philippians 3:8

   Philippians 3:13b–14

   Philippians 4:8

Philippians 4:19–20

THINK IT THROUGH AND STORE IT UP

4. In what ways has your faith awakened to the treasure of Christ as you have worked through this study? How are you experiencing revival in your soul as a result?

5. Are you experiencing the absolute treasure of Christ? What does this mean to you? How is this transforming your life?

6. Did you accomplish the goals you set for yourself in week one? If yes, how so? If not, what do you still need to do to hit your mark?

7. What is/are your greatest takeaway(s) from this study?

8. You have spent the last ten weeks reading, studying, and discussing the book of Philippians. You've been taking it in, writing it down, thinking it through, and storing it up. In what specific ways are you planning to make it count?

AWAKEN MY HEART: A CLOSING PRAYER

You are the all-sovereign God.
You are the all-knowing God.
You are the all-sufficient God.

You are faithful. You are good. You are kind.
You are Jesus: my portion, my inheritance, my eternal reward.
Awaken my heart and revive my soul.

Your greatness is incomprehensible.
Your fullness inexhaustible.
Your riches unsearchable.

Your love extends, your grace abounds, your truth prevails.
You are my Savior, my Lord, my God.
Awaken my heart and revive my soul.

You are the breath in my lungs,
The energy in my work,
The provider of my needs.

You are my satisfaction, my joy, and my crown.
You are the Christ who loves me, saves me, and keeps me.
Awaken my heart and revive my soul.

Your faithfulness astounds me.
Your peace surrounds me.
Your embrace awaits me.

You are my One thing, my heart's desire, the lover of my soul.
You are Yahweh—absolutely everything to me.
Awaken my heart and revive my soul.

You are my greatest treasure.
I love you with all that I am.
All my days, God, awaken my heart and revive my soul
In the fullness of you, Jesus my Lord.

Your name be praised forever and ever.

Amen.

AWAKEN

PHILIPPIANS

English Standard Version

1 Paul and Timothy, servants of Christ Jesus, To all the saints in Christ Jesus who are at Philippi, with the overseers and deacons: ² Grace to you and peace from God our Father and the Lord Jesus Christ.

³ I thank my God in all my remembrance of you, ⁴ always in every prayer of mine for you all making my prayer with joy, ⁵ because of your partnership in the gospel from the first day until now. ⁶ And I am sure of this, that he who began a good work in you will bring it to completion at the day of Jesus Christ.

⁷ It is right for me to feel this way about you all, because I hold you in my heart, for you are all partakers with me of grace, both in my imprisonment and in the defense and confirmation of the gospel. ⁸ For God is my witness, how I yearn for you all with the affection of Christ Jesus.

⁹ And it is my prayer that your love may abound more and more, with knowledge and all discernment, ¹⁰ so that you may approve what is excellent, and so be pure and blameless for the day of Christ, ¹¹ filled with the fruit of righteousness that comes through Jesus Christ, to the glory and praise of God.

¹² I want you to know, brothers, that what has happened to me has really served to advance the gospel, ¹³ so that it has become known throughout the whole imperial guard and to all the rest that my imprisonment is for Christ. ¹⁴ And most of the brothers, having become confident in the Lord by my imprisonment, are much more bold to speak the word without fear. ¹⁵ Some indeed preach Christ from envy and rivalry, but others from good will. ¹⁶ The latter do it out of love, knowing that I am put here for the defense of the gospel. ¹⁷ The former proclaim Christ out of selfish ambition, not sincerely but thinking to afflict me in

my imprisonment. [18] What then? Only that in every way, whether in pretense or in truth, Christ is proclaimed, and in that I rejoice. Yes, and I will rejoice,

[19] for I know that through your prayers and the help of the Spirit of Jesus Christ this will turn out for my deliverance, [20] as it is my eager expectation and hope that I will not be at all ashamed, but that with full courage now as always Christ will be honored in my body, whether by life or by death. [21] For to me to live is Christ, and to die is gain. [22] If I am to live in the flesh, that means fruitful labor for me. Yet which I shall choose I cannot tell. [23] I am hard pressed between the two. My desire is to depart and be with Christ, for that is far better. [24] But to remain in the flesh is more necessary on your account. [25] Convinced of this, I know that I will remain and continue with you all, for your progress and joy in the faith, [26] so that in me you may have ample cause to glory in Christ Jesus, because of my coming to you again.

[27] Only let your manner of life be worthy of the gospel of Christ, so that whether I come and see you or am absent, I may hear of you that you are standing firm in one spirit, with one mind striving side by side for the faith of the gospel, [28] and not frightened in anything by your opponents. This is a clear sign to them of their destruction, but of your salvation, and that from God. [29] For it has been granted to you that for the sake of Christ you should not only believe in him but also suffer for his sake, [30] engaged in the same conflict that you saw I had and now hear that I still have.

2 So if there is any encouragement in Christ, any comfort from love, any participation in the Spirit, any affection and sympathy, [2] complete my joy by being of the same mind, having the same love, being in full accord and of one mind. [3] Do nothing from selfish ambition or conceit, but in humility count others more significant than yourselves. [4] Let each of you look not only to his own interests, but also to the interests of others.

⁵ Have this mind among yourselves, which is yours in Christ Jesus, ⁶ who, though he was in the form of God, did not count equality with God a thing to be grasped, ⁷ but emptied himself, by taking the form of a servant, being born in the likeness of men. ⁸ And being found in human form, he humbled himself by becoming obedient to the point of death, even death on a cross.

⁹ Therefore God has highly exalted him and bestowed on him the name that is above every name, ¹⁰ so that at the name of Jesus every knee should bow, in heaven and on earth and under the earth, ¹¹ and every tongue confess that Jesus Christ is Lord, to the glory of God the Father.

¹² Therefore, my beloved, as you have always obeyed, so now, not only as in my presence but much more in my absence, work out your own salvation with fear and trembling, ¹³ for it is God who works in you, both to will and to work for his good pleasure. ¹⁴ Do all things without grumbling or disputing, ¹⁵ that you may be blameless and innocent, children of God without blemish in the midst of a crooked and twisted generation, among whom you shine as lights in the world, ¹⁶ holding fast to the word of life, so that in the day of Christ I may be proud that I did not run in vain or labor in vain. ¹⁷ Even if I am to be poured out as a drink offering upon the sacrificial offering of your faith, I am glad and rejoice with you all. ¹⁸ Likewise you also should be glad and rejoice with me.

¹⁹ I hope in the Lord Jesus to send Timothy to you soon, so that I too may be cheered by news of you. ²⁰ For I have no one like him, who will be genuinely concerned for your welfare. ²¹ For they all seek their own interests, not those of Jesus Christ. ²² But you know Timothy's proven worth, how as a son with a father he has served with me in the gospel. ²³ I hope therefore to send him just as soon as I see how it will go with me, ²⁴ and I trust in the Lord that shortly I myself will come also.

[25] I have thought it necessary to send to you Epaphroditus my brother and fellow worker and fellow soldier, and your messenger and minister to my need, [26] for he has been longing for you all and has been distressed because you heard that he was ill. [27] Indeed he was ill, near to death. But God had mercy on him, and not only on him but on me also, lest I should have sorrow upon sorrow. [28] I am the more eager to send him, therefore, that you may rejoice at seeing him again, and that I may be less anxious. [29] So receive him in the Lord with all joy, and honor such men, [30] for he nearly died for the work of Christ, risking his life to complete what was lacking in your service to me.

3 Finally, my brothers, rejoice in the Lord. To write the same things to you is no trouble to me and is safe for you. [2] Look out for the dogs, look out for the evildoers, look out for those who mutilate the flesh. [3] For we are the circumcision, who worship by the Spirit of God and glory in Christ Jesus and put no confidence in the flesh—

[4] though I myself have reason for confidence in the flesh also. If anyone else thinks he has reason for confidence in the flesh, I have more: [5] circumcised on the eighth day, of the people of Israel, of the tribe of Benjamin, a Hebrew of Hebrews; as to the law, a Pharisee; [6] as to zeal, a persecutor of the church; as to righteousness under the law, blameless. [7] But whatever gain I had, I counted as loss for the sake of Christ. [8] Indeed, I count everything as loss because of the surpassing worth of knowing Christ Jesus my Lord. For his sake I have suffered the loss of all things and count them as rubbish, in order that I may gain Christ [9] and be found in him, not having a righteousness of my own that comes from the law, but that which comes through faith in Christ, the righteousness from God that depends on faith— [10] that I may know him and the power of his resurrection, and may share his sufferings, becoming like him in his death, [11] that by any means possible I may attain the resurrection from the dead.

¹² Not that I have already obtained this or am already perfect, but I press on to make it my own, because Christ Jesus has made me his own. ¹³ Brothers, I do not consider that I have made it my own. But one thing I do: forgetting what lies behind and straining forward to what lies ahead, ¹⁴ I press on toward the goal for the prize of the upward call of God in Christ Jesus. ¹⁵ Let those of us who are mature think this way, and if in anything you think otherwise, God will reveal that also to you. ¹⁶ Only let us hold true to what we have attained.

¹⁷ Brothers, join in imitating me, and keep your eyes on those who walk according to the example you have in us. ¹⁸ For many, of whom I have often told you and now tell you even with tears, walk as enemies of the cross of Christ. ¹⁹ Their end is destruction, their god is their belly, and they glory in their shame, with minds set on earthly things.

²⁰ But our citizenship is in heaven, and from it we await a Savior, the Lord Jesus Christ, ²¹ who will transform our lowly body to be like his glorious body, by the power that enables him even to subject all things to himself. **4** Therefore, my brothers, whom I love and long for, my joy and crown, stand firm thus in the Lord, my beloved.

² I entreat Euodia and I entreat Syntyche to agree in the Lord. ³ Yes, I ask you also, true companion, help these women, who have labored side by side with me in the gospel together with Clement and the rest of my fellow workers, whose names are in the book of life.

⁴ Rejoice in the Lord always; again I will say, rejoice. ⁵ Let your reasonableness be known to everyone. The Lord is at hand; ⁶ do not be anxious about anything, but in everything by prayer and supplication with thanksgiving let your requests be made known to God. ⁷ And the peace of God, which surpasses all understanding, will guard your hearts and your minds in Christ Jesus.

⁸ Finally, brothers, whatever is true, whatever is honorable, whatever is just, whatever is pure, whatever is lovely, whatever is commendable, if there is any excellence, if there is anything worthy of praise, think about these things. ⁹ What you have learned and received and heard and seen in me—practice these things, and the God of peace will be with you.

¹⁰ I rejoiced in the Lord greatly that now at length you have revived your concern for me. You were indeed concerned for me, but you had no opportunity. ¹¹ Not that I am speaking of being in need, for I have learned in whatever situation I am to be content. ¹² I know how to be brought low, and I know how to abound. In any and every circumstance, I have learned the secret of facing plenty and hunger, abundance and need. ¹³ I can do all things through him who strengthens me.

¹⁴ Yet it was kind of you to share my trouble. ¹⁵ And you Philippians yourselves know that in the beginning of the gospel, when I left Macedonia, no church entered into partnership with me in giving and receiving, except you only. ¹⁶ Even in Thessalonica you sent me help for my needs once and again. ¹⁷ Not that I seek the gift, but I seek the fruit that increases to your credit. ¹⁸ I have received full payment, and more. I am well supplied, having received from Epaphroditus the gifts you sent, a fragrant offering, a sacrifice acceptable and pleasing to God. ¹⁹ And my God will supply every need of yours according to his riches in glory in Christ Jesus.

²⁰ To our God and Father be glory forever and ever. Amen. ²¹ Greet every saint in Christ Jesus. The brothers who are with me greet you. ²² All the saints greet you, especially those of Caesar's household. ²³ The grace of the Lord Jesus Christ be with your spirit.

WORD STUDIES[24]

Word	Text	Strong's #	Greek Word	Definition
Week One				
servant	1:1	1401	*doulos*	slave, devoted to another to the disregard of one's own interests
grace	1:2	5485	*charis*	merciful kindness, undeserved favor of God, that which affords joy
peace	1:2	1515	*eireēnē*	rest, quietness of soul, assured salvation through Christ
Week Two				
joy	1:4	5479	*chara*	calm delight, inner exuberance
partnership	1:5	2842	*koinōnia*	fellowship, joint participation, community
partakers	1:7	4791	*sygkoinōnos*	companion, joint partner
affection	1:8	4698	*splagchnon*	bowels, inward affection
abound	1:9	4052	*perisseuō*	exceed, in abundance, overflow
discernment	1:9	144	*aisthēsis*	perception, judgment, cognition
approve	1:10	1381	*dokimazō*	to examine and recognize as genuine
Week Three				
live	1:21	2198	*zaō*	breathe, be alive, enjoy real life

| standing firm | 1:27 | 4739 | *stēkō* | persevere, persist, anchored in place |

Week Four
Humility	2:3	5012	*tapeinophrosynē*	humble opinion of oneself, modesty; awareness of one's smallness
emptied	2:7	2758	*kenoō*	make void, make of no reputation, set aside
exalted	2:9	5251	*hyperypsoō*	raise to highest rank and power, to extol most highly
Lord	2:11	2962	*kyrios*	master, supreme in authority, title given to God

Week Five
lights	2:15	5458	*phōstēr*	luminary, brightness, brilliancy
like him	2:20	2473	*isopsychos*	like-minded, equal in soul Literal: of kindred spirit
be concerned	2:20	3309	*merimnaō*	to be anxious, to care for, look out for

Week Six
rejoice	3:1	5463	*chairō*	be glad, exude exceeding joy, thrive
gain	3:7	2771(noun)	*kerdos*	advantage
rubbish	3:8	4657	*skybalon*	garbage, dung, worthless and detestable
righteousness	3:9	1343	*dikaiosynē*	condition acceptable to God, integrity, purity of life and character

Week Seven

press on	3:12	1377	*diōkō*	follow after, pursue, seek after eagerly, earnestly endeavor to acquire

Week Eight

entreat	4:2	3870	*parakaleō*	urge, beg, admonish, exhort
reasonableness	4:5	1933	*epieikēs*	gentle spirit, fair, mild
anxious	4:6	3309	*merimnaō*	troubled with cares, burdened with worry

Week Nine

revive	4:10	330	*anathallō*	shoot, sprout up again, flourish again
saints	4:21	40	*hagios*	most holy things, sacred

NOTES

[1] Matthew Bridges, "Crown Him With Many Crowns," *Choice Hymns of the Faith* (Ft. Dodge, IA: Gospel Perpetuating Fund, 1944), 10.

[2] William P. MacKay, "Revive Us Again," *Abiding Songs* (Nashville, TN: Sunday School Board of the Southern Baptist Convention, 1936), d143.

[3] Steven J. Lawson, *Philippians For You* (Charlotte, NC: The Good Book Company, 2017), 39.

[4] F.F. Bruce, *Philippians* (Peabody, MA: Hendrickson Publishers, Inc., 1989), 31.

[5] John H. Sammis, "Trust and Obey," *Choice Hymns of the Faith* (Ft. Dodge, IA: Gospel Perpetuating Fund, 1944), 319.

[6] Bruce, *Philippians*, 48.

[7] "Q & A 1," *The Heidelberg Catechism* (Christian Reformed Church, 2004), Print.

[8] Matt Chandler, *To Live is Christ* (Colorado Springs: David C Cook, 2013), 45.

[9] Chandler, To Live is Christ, 64.

[10] Joachim Neander, Translator Catherine Winkworth, "Praise to the Lord, the Almighty," *Hymns and Songs for the Sunday School* (Philadelphia: The Lutheran Publication Society, 1914), 37.

[11] Lawson, *Philippians For You*, 89.

[12] Chandler, *To Live is Christ*, 76.

[13] Wilkinson, Kate B. "May the Mind of Christ My Savior," (1925), Hymnary.org. Accessed October 1, 2022.

[14] Warren Wiersbe, *The Wiersbe Bible Commentary* (Colorado Springs: David C Cook, 2007), 641.

[15] Charles Wesley, "Love Divine, All Loves Excelling," *A Collection of Hymns* (New York: G. Lane & C.B. Tippett, 1845), 310.

[16] Wiersbe, *The Wiersbe Bible Commentary*, 645.

[17] Lawson, *Philippians For You*, 139.

[18] Chandler, *To Live is Christ*, 95.

[19] William R. Featherstone, "My Jesus I Love Thee," *Abiding Faith* (Dayton, TN: R.E. Winsett, 1947), 97.

[20] Johnson Oatman, Jr. "Higher Ground," *Alexander's Hymns No. 3* (Wheaton, IL: Fleming H. Revell Company, 1915), 165.

[21] Chandler, *To Live is Christ*, 148.

[22] Gerald F. Hawthorne and Ralph P. Martin, *Philippians* (Grand Rapids, MI: Thomas Nelson, Inc., 2004), 246.

[23] Stephen Ganschow, PhD.

[24] Henry VanDyke, "Joyful, Joyful, We Adore Thee," *Alleluia* (Santa Ana, CA: The Westminster Press, 1916), 198.

[25] Thomas O. Chisholm, "Great is Thy Faithfulness," *Christian Worship,* (Philadelphia: Judson Press, 1941), 165.

[26] Author's paraphrase of Blueletterbible.org definitions